Accolades for *Are You Fit to Love?*

The most daring and life-changing relationship book I have ever read!
 —Ursula Summ

Delightful and inspiring, Are You Fit to Love? *sheds new light on one of the core issues of human existence—relationships. Self-realization and self-gratification have become key words in a society that encourages a self-focused lifestyle. Yet more people than ever feel alone and lonely, as many are unable to form lasting and mutually supportive relationships.*

With humor and passion, author Allie Ochs reminds us that being in a relationship is all about being with another. In **Are You Fit to Love?***, she explores the qualities that are the key ingredients of any successful relationship, and lovingly shares them through the insights and wisdom of personal **and professional** experience.*

For all who have looked for, but not found, **true** *happiness in their relationships,* **Are You Fit to Love?** *is a lifeline worth grabbing!*
 —Simone Gabbay

Timing is everything! **Are You Fit to Love?** *came along at a perfect time to get our 35 year marriage back on track. It served to help us regain objectivity and therefore empathy for our respective points of view. The longer a marriage lasts, the more it needs a "Refresher" course like this.*
 —Samm Coombs

Are You Fit to Love? *with it's distinctive voice and brilliant angle is an unparalleled solution to our relationship turmoils whether we are single or not!*
—David Fullerton

Guys get as tired of revolving door relationships as I expect women do. I've gone with women who were marrying material. But maybe there was the super woman around the next corner. You see the problem, because you laid out the solution in your book. Next time, I'll take your advice and "go for it."
—Richard Miller

Are You Fit to Love? *provides a dramatic, revolutionary, yet surprisingly simple solution to our international relationship disease of broken hearts and shattered dreams. This is a very intelligent and entertaining Must Read!*
—Sherrie Slack

My third marriage was about to go down the drain; his second. I'd been through the counseling bit to no avail. So I read **Are You Fit to Love?** *And guess what? Neither of us were, but now we are trying to be. What a difference your book made.*
—M. Mueller

ARE YOU FIT TO LOVE?

ARE YOU FIT TO LOVE?

A RADICALLY DIFFERENT APPROACH TO SUCCESSFUL RELATIONSHIPS

Allie Ochs

LITTLE MOOSE PRESS
Beverly Hills, CA, USA

ARE YOU FIT TO LOVE?
A Radically Different Approach to Successful Relationships
By Allie Ochs

Copyright © 2003 Allie Ochs

All rights reserved. No part of this book may be reproduced or transmitted in any form or by any means, electronic or mechanical, including photocopying, recording, or by any information storage and retrieval system, without permission in writing from the publisher.

Published by

275 South Beverly Drive, Suite 100
Beverly Hills, CA 90212
310-278-6239 Fax: 310-278-6238
toll free: 866-234-0626
info@littlemoosepress.com
www.littlemoosepress.com
mailing address:
269 So. Beverly Drive #1065
Beverly Hills, CA 90212

First Edition
ISBN 0972022791
Library of Congress Control Number: 2003111724
SAN 254-9778
$15.95 U.S.
$19.95 Canada

Publisher's Cataloging-in-Publication Data available upon request.

Printed and bound in the United States of America

Book Design: Dotti Albertine
Cover Photograph: Robert Hankins

To my daughter, Nina

She is my inspiration, my friend, my teacher and supporter. My journey to unconditional love began with her and throughout the years I have become a better person because of her. She awakened my heart, so that I may love all of humankind.

*The hope of the world lies
in what one demands,
not of others, but of oneself.*
—James Baldwin (1924–1987)

Acknowledgements

Over the past four years my family, friends and even strangers have given their love and time to the completion of this book, beginning with my dear friend, Beverly, without whom this book would have never happened. When I was lost she showed me the way and her abundant love is like a solid anchor in my life. I thank Ulla for 30 years of a meaningful and truthful friendship. I would like to thank my daughter Nina for being completely selfless and independent, allowing me to dedicate my time and energies to this book. I thank my father, who taught me the countless life skills required to complete this project. I am especially grateful to David, who lived daily with me through the trials and tribulations of writing and publishing.

And heartfelt thanks to my professors at the University of Western Ontario for their encouragement, feedback and resources. Also, thank you Simone Gabbay for your pre-edit, advice and compassion. Likewise to Susana Gomes.

I must also extend my appreciation to Ellen Reid, my book shepherd, who steered me through the mysteries of converting a manuscript into a book that seeks its proper level in the marketplace. Special thanks to my in-house "Devils" editor, Samm Coombs, who helped me be objective about the subjective.

Last, but not least, I'd like to thank all who shared their experiences, feelings, deepest secrets and love, be they in, out of or almost in a relationship. Their contributions are the backbone of this book.

About the Book

*I*nterpersonal relationships make the "world go round"—yet our epidemic inability to "get along" has become the root cause of failed marriages and short-lived romantic liaisons. It's no surprise that partnerships fall apart with the old "blame game" at work. Most of us are totally inept when it comes to being objective and constructive; never knowing what it takes to engender lasting, fulfilling and mutually supportive relationships.

The author, Allie Ochs, not only manages to untangle the relationship webs we weave; she achieves the larger task of laying out the key ingredients for all successful relationships. She accomplishes this with the empathy and wisdom of someone who has "been there." Raised in a dysfunctional family and having suffered her own failed marriage, she went on to work in the singles and personal introduction industry. The foregoing, combined with her academic studies, led to her life's work as a professional Interpersonal Relationship Coach.

Are You Fit to Love? takes a radically different approach than so many self-help manuals with their step-by-step programs, scripted interactions and staged behavior. While the book's two guiding tenets—*mutual respect* and *moral responsibility*—are simple enough at face value; Ms. Ochs adopts a proactive, street-wise approach for practicing these principles. Thus you'll read why men and women are *not* different, why you must put all your eggs in one basket, why there are many right people for you, why sex clouds your judgment, why your ego interferes with love. These and so many other "whys" lead to the much more important "how-to's" including how to make insecurity disappear, how to avoid control games, how to stop resenting each other, how to give someone a chance, how to prevent an affair, how to know when to "go for it" and when to quit. The reader will come to recognize the difference between half-hearted and whole-hearted; why there is no conflict between selflessness and self-esteem.

Many a book promises to be a life-changing medium. *Are You Fit to Love?* delivers, albeit with certain provisos: The author's prescriptions will prove efficacious only if the reader has an open mind and a determination to seek a lasting relationship. It will also help that you are sick and tired of being alone.

ABOUT THE AUTHOR

Anyone who counsels on "matters of the heart" should possess three essential credentials: **empathy, savvy** and **education**. Allie Ochs developed **empathy**, the ability to emotionally relate to another's situation, through "the school of hard knocks" where she experienced the emotional turbulence of failed relationships. Growing up in a family decimated by divorce and abuse, followed by her own divorce, she endured ensuing stormy relationships and the hardship of single parenthood. Allie Ochs is very capable of walking every mile in the shoes of those with similar painful histories.

Allie acquired the second credential, **savvy**, by applying her personal experience and knowledge in a professional capacity. She converted her Ontario farm into a retreat where she conducted seminars for private and corporate clients. Her popular "Joy Of Living" program centered on how to stop focusing on what we lack and unleash the best within us. Allie Ochs also worked as a relationships counselor for the Canadian division of the largest international matchmaking firm.

This background persuaded her to acquire the third credential, **education.** She attended the University of Western Ontario full time to study psychology, sociology and philosophy. These credentials combined with five years of research and interviews qualify Allie to offer new insights and techniques for "finding and keeping true love." *Are You Fit to Love?* involved enormous introspection to address such an emotionally charged subject and to offer a brilliant angle on relationships unavailable elsewhere.

Currently Allie is working on her new book: *Are You Fit to Parent?* while still coaching interpersonal relationships that are central to all aspects of our lives.

A German national, Allie Ochs immigrated to Canada in 1981. Prior to her current career she owned and operated a dairy farm with her then-husband. Following her divorce she became a pioneer in the emu breeding business and also raised horses. She holds a number of business management and marketing diplomas from the Chamber of Industry and Commerce (Germany), Fanshaw College and the Business Development Bank in Canada.

CONTENTS

CHAPTER 1

OFF-AND-ON SINGLE, ALMOST SINGLE OR MARRIED   17
Straight Facts and Uplifting Accounts of the Jerks and Junkies

- Single or Married: Often a Minute Distinction?   18
- Married: Half-Heartedly Involved or Sentenced for Life?   19
- Off-and-On Single and Almost Single   24
- Road-kill on the Singles Super Highway   27
- Internet Dating Services in a Nutshell   32
- Matching Agencies   33
- The New Generation of Senior Singles   36

CHAPTER 2

GARAGE SALE FOR SINGLES   39
The New, Used and Abused

- The New   40
- The Used   41
- The Abused   42
- Who Stopped the Payment on our Reality Check?   43
- The Emotionally Healthy Person   44
- Someone's Garbage is Somebody Else's Treasure   48

CHAPTER 3

ARE WOMEN FROM UTOPIA AND MEN FROM WAL-MART?   53
Physical Differences vs. Human Commonalities

- The Division of the Blues and the Pinks   54
- Society Has Played a Trick on Us   56
- The Menstruating Pilot and the Male Mother   58
- The Opposite Sex is No Mystery   61

CHAPTER 4

DRIVING SCHOOL FOR SINGLES   **67**
Choosing the Right Gear

- ❤ Stuck in Park and Reverse   68
- ❤ Permanent Single-ism   72
- ❤ Drive   78
- ❤ Learning the "Trade of Love" Instead of the "Tricks"   79

CHAPTER 5

LOOKING OVER THE SHOULDER   **83**
Commitment Until Something Better Comes Along

- ❤ I Love You Because I Don't Know You   85
- ❤ Cover Me! I Am Changing Lanes   89
- ❤ The Human Spirit Can Never Commit to a Compromise   91
- ❤ Choose Your Love and Love Your Choice   93
- ❤ Making Love a Priority   99

CHAPTER 6

LOVE McDONALD'S STYLE   **101**
Fast, Cheap and Easy

- ❤ McChicks and McStuds at the "All-You-Can-Eat" Buffet   102
- ❤ Shall Birds of a Feather Flock Together?   107
- ❤ Dumb Founded   110
- ❤ Attitude Adjustment   114
- ❤ Love at First Bite   116

CHAPTER 7

I LOVE ME; WHOM DO YOU LOVE?   **125**
If I Love You, Will I Get the Goody Bag?

- ❤ If Life Is a Game, Let's Change the Rules   126
- ❤ I Love You if You Love Me First   129
- ❤ Conflict and Control   133

- Fear, a Life-Bandit — 143
- Who Will Get a Clean Bill of Emotional Health? — 150
- Why We Feel Inadequate — 155

CHAPTER 8

WE WERE BORN NAKED, WET AND HUNGRY AND THEN IT GOT WORSE — 161
There Is No Reality, Only Perception

- It Is as Bad as You Think It Is and They Are out to Get You — 163
- It Is Entirely Their Fault — 167
- Thinking: *No matter how thin you slice it, there are always two sides* — 170
- Communicating: *I am listening, but I can't hear you* — 173
- Assuming: *I know so much less than there is to know* — 178

CHAPTER 9

SEX *Versus* MAKING LOVE — 181
From Failing Hard Drives to Floating Silicone Devices

- Turning Our Lives Over to Hormones — 181
- A Sex-Saturated Population — 184
- Sexual Dysfunction versus Dissatisfaction — 185
- We Are All Natural Experts at Sex — 192
- Making Love: *Revealing the fragile self* — 199

CHAPTER 10

WHAT IS THIS THING CALLED LOVE? — 209
Love is a Choice: *Choose It or Lose It*

- Unconditional Love — 216
- Love, the Universal Cure — 220
- Conclusion — 224

CHAPTER 1

OFF-AND-ON SINGLE / ALMOST SINGLE / OR MARRIED
Straight Facts and Uplifting Accounts of the Jerks and Junkies

> *If love is not a game, why are there so many players?*
> —ALLIE OCHS

THE FIRST DIVORCE in my family was my parents', followed by the divorce of my grandmother, that of my aunt, and later that of my uncle. It is almost as if my parents' divorce triggered a whole chain of family divorces. My younger brother was next in line, then it was my turn, and eventually my older brother divorced, too.

During those years of family divorces, strange things happened. My younger brother lived in a common-law relationship with the ex-wife of the new boyfriend of my ex-sister-in-law (are you lost yet?). My former husband's second ex-wife (who fell in love with his best friend) and I involuntarily became neighbors. My older brother lived with his ex-wife's best friend. My mother married the father of my ex-husband's brother-in-law. Nobody was ever really sure where the children or the pets of these relationships would eventually land.

I call these triangles of relationships *love-extinctions* on the fast track. You can see how mutable the status of single, married, or almost single is and how easily relations change within a narrow circle. This is just one family's example. Fortunately, everyone survived unharmed and unarmed.

Given the fact that my family was anything but perfect, it is rather obvious that I am not perfect myself. You are about to read an imperfect book by an imperfect writer about imperfect relationships. However, this book will deliver the most paramount answers about relationships and save you from years of despair and therapy. If, after reading this book, you still find yourself unable to find or improve a relationship, you may have to read it again.

❤ Single or Married — Often a Minute Distinction

Traditionally, married status describes those who have gone through a civil and/or religious ceremony, who live together with or without children, and who promised to part only on death. Single status, on the other hand, often implies being without a partner by choice or failure. Being single evokes notions of dating services, singles bars, and Internet romances, which are still assigned a "meat-market" stigma. In our couple-oriented society, being single often conjures up images of failed relationships or undesirability. Singles are sometimes also feared as a threat to established relationships.

More than ever, our adult population is cycling from the status of single to married to divorced and back to single again, often repeating this cycle. While single and married persons belong to distinct groups with specific assumptions about their members, the distinction has become blurred to the point where relationships may be considered hybrids of single or married. Awareness of these hybrids and the reasons for their often speedy transitions can help change us from being someone who wanders from one relationship to another into someone with a whole new perspective.

❤ Married: Half-Heartedly Involved or Sentenced for Life

The fantasy of being with someone else is just one of many characteristics of half-heartedness. Other examples are a lack of honest communication, a lack of intimacy, or the failure to appreciate the other person as a whole. Such unions clearly lack *mutual respect* and *moral responsibility* that are the key components of any meaningful relationship—though they are often poorly understood. Today, *mutual respect* has become so eroded that often one partner barely acknowledges the other's feelings, values, and beliefs. This erosion is a far cry from *mutual respect*.

Moral responsibility is practiced only if it does not interfere with our own gratification, and we ignore the fact that all our actions affect those around us. We often rationalize immoral and disrespectful behavior by blaming our partners for not meeting our needs. We invent new ways to make our partners pay for their shortcomings. All of these actions only serve to build resentment. We could solve almost all our relationship problems by understanding and applying the concepts of *mutual respect* and *moral responsibility*. These are the two most important relationship principles. Regardless of where you find yourself in your current relationship, or however unsuccessfully you have tried to establish a relationship, *mutual respect* and *moral responsibility* is where it all begins.

The fundamental concept of marriage is commitment to a spouse and romantic unavailability to anyone else. When married couples have different interpretations of marriage, one or both of the spouses may become half-heartedly involved. The salient experiences of being half-heartedly involved are disconnectedness from the partner as well as second-guessing one's choice of partner. Some feel disconnected occasionally, while others feel it more frequently or even all the time. (No, this has nothing to do with PMS or mid-life crisis!) People find many reasons to justify such feelings at one point or another during their marriage. Most of these reasons reflect the pattern of a society whose members are losing sight of the fact that they are indeed responsible for everything they feel, do, say, and think.

Do those who are half-heartedly involved have affairs? Some have long-term affairs with the same person, others have affairs with several partners, and some may cheat just once. Sadly, the commandment, *Thou shall not commit adultery* has been twisted into *Thou shall not admit adultery*. There are those who never cheat but keep the fantasy of doing so alive. Almost 50 percent of married people have affairs. Slightly over 70 percent are dissatisfied with their sex life, and 85 percent wish for more romance. Far too many married people entertain thoughts of someone else, and some even believe this to be normal. This is illustrated by the example of Pierre, a regular at the local strip joint. His wife, Claire, felt hurt, but Pierre thought nothing of frequenting such places for stimulation. Pierre defended his ritual with the argument that many other men visited such establishments as well. In fact, he enjoyed flirting with other women and never missed a *Playboy* issue, yet failed to understand why Claire was so offended. Ultimately, Pierre even had an affair. It is no secret that numerous men and an increasing number of women seek excitement outside of their relationship, but there are still many who do not. Claire eventually left Pierre because she wanted to be with someone who was wholeheartedly involved with her.

Is it possible to be attracted to someone else, yet still love your partner? Many feel that it is, and some even feel justified in acting upon their attraction. Being attracted to someone is easily confused with finding someone else attractive. There is often the illusion that another person could provide elements that are perceived to be lacking in the relationship. However, when you truly respect your partner you will not allow desire to surface and you will not engage in blatant betrayal or demoralizing behavior by "fantasizing about" or even "pursuing" another person. You will treat your partner exactly the way you want to be treated. In simple terms, if you long for a life partner who is wholeheartedly behind you, you must throw your whole heart into the relationship. Ironically, many lack in a relationship that which they themselves fail to provide, as the following examples demonstrate:

Brandon feels that Gina resents his passion for race-cars. She constantly complains about stumbling over car parts while she expects him to tolerate falling over her house pets which he didn't want in the first place. They are literally stumbling over each other's passions while resenting each other for not respecting their own pursuits. Since they have both, car parts and pets, wouldn't it make sense to respect each other's interests?

If we want understanding in our relationships, we must set the example of being understanding ourselves. If this sounds more like giving than receiving, you are probably right, because giving is the cause of receiving.

A woman who complains that her boyfriend doesn't listen to her may not be listening to him. Often our partners are not listening to us because we ourselves fail to listen attentively. A man, who complains to his wife that their children seem more important to her than he is, might want to ask himself if there isn't something in his life which takes priority over her.

If we fall short in making our mates a priority, we should not be surprised if it backfires. Our relationships could be significantly improved if we reflected on our own shortcomings before blaming our partner.

When you are half-heartedly involved, a vital part of you is absent. While putting all your eggs in one basket is not a good policy in financial investments, it is essential for relationships. When only a part of you is invested, your partner will sense it. This type of situation creates a *go-nowhere-energy* in relationships. Both of you may come to feel sentenced for life, helpless, and unable to give your relationship new meaning. You may become apathetic and see yourselves as victims of circumstances beyond your control. If you are in a relationship fueled by *go-nowhere-energy*, you must realize that you have contributed to these circumstances.

Why are so many people half-heartedly engaged, and why are they changing their status more often than at any other time in history? The answer lies in the dramatic changes in a society that is evolving faster than ever before. The role shift of men and women has had far-reaching implications in terms of how we relate to one another in every area of our lives. The changes of many traditional guidelines have redefined our relationships and produced incredible turmoil and uncertainty in our intimate unions.

While conventional customs, values, gender roles, and religious conviction defined the boundaries for relationships of the past, no previous generation has contemplated life the way we do. No previous generation has searched for deeper meaning, sought to heal childhood wounds, or coped with "baggage" from previous relationships. No previous generation has had its desires awakened with the prospect of instant gratification, and then elevated individual fulfillment above all else, insisting that we can have it all while contributing so poorly to our relationships.

In our search for gratification and happiness, our expectations have become elevated, while most of the traditional relationship boundaries of previous generations have been removed. When it comes to relationships, we are convinced that we deserve it all. We demand immediate payoffs and often no longer have the patience to stick around for long-term gains.

It is no surprise that the divorce rate has reached an alarming high. On average, new marriages last slightly over two years, and one out of every three adults is expected to be single by the end of this decade. This projects a sad image of emotional disconnectedness for nearly half of the adult population. Not only are we failing in our attempts to find and maintain loyal, committed relationships of *mutual respect* and *moral responsibility*, but we are also failing our children. In fact, we provide a blueprint for failure by teaching "that anything goes."

> *While we try to teach our children all about life,*
> *our children teach us what life is all about.*
> — ANGELA SCHWINDT

In view of this gloomy picture, we become obsessed with the ingredients for the ideal relationship, and we are reading and listening to all sorts of advice, often without making significant positive changes. In our quest for self-discovery, we fail to ask these important questions: *Am I the person I ought to be? Am I fit to love?* If we want to find truly meaningful relationships, we must first ensure that we can answer yes to both questions.

If there is disappointment in a marriage, it is almost never solely one spouse's fault. While most people marry with the sincerest intentions, more is required to make the marriage work. Everyone who enters into marriage should be clear about the terms of commitment to each other. Each must be able to say to the other:

1. I respect you as I do myself. (If you are unsure about the meaning of mutual, this is it.)

2. I am morally responsible for all of my actions and their consequences upon you.

3. There will be no problems in this marriage — only a lack of solutions!

4. The least important word in my vocabulary will be "I," and the most important word will be "we."

5. I will do as I say and mean what I say.

6. If I should commit adultery, I will give you all our joint assets, let you leave with the children, and support you as you establish your new life.

7. If we should break our contract of loving each other until death parts us, we both agree to throw an all-expenses-paid divorce party for all guests who attended our wedding. At this time, we will return all wedding gifts that we received, including gifts of cash.

Everything should be made as simple as possible — but no simpler.
—ALBERT EINSTEIN

❤ Off-and-On Single and Almost Single

Even if you are in a relationship, you will benefit from reading this section and other discussions about singles because there is a 50 percent chance of your joining the singles scene sooner or later. Furthermore, you will discover how to prevent your relationship from becoming a statistic by applying the principles of *mutual respect* and *moral responsibility*.

As already suggested, people often change their single status from on to off in the blink of an eye, or become almost single and ready to harvest a better crop. In reality, there is not much difference between those who are in an emotionally distant relationship and those who are almost single. Almost-singles are in relationships but pretend to be single if an opportunity promises a better yield, even if only for a short duration.

The number of singles is rising, and being single has been elevated to the point of being a socially acceptable or even desirable lifestyle. More and more younger women are postponing marriage in favor of their careers. The highest proportion of never-married people can be found in the category of professional, well-educated women. Many of these women welcome the glorified solo-lifestyle. Because of their economic independence, they no longer seek financial security from a man. Instead, some seek relationships that provide emotional support, personal fulfillment, and intellectual challenge. Others prefer to maintain casual relationships without any strings attached. This new breed of women, whose attitudes about relationships resemble those historically ascribed to men, confuses single men. Younger, never-married singles tend to marry at older ages and less frequently than in previous generations.

It is a personal choice to live in a common-law relationship or to be married. In either case, however, we are often focused on how to end the relationship as soon as it begins. Paradoxically, many people promise to love their partners until their last breath, while simultaneously negotiating a marriage contract that sets out the fine details of when and how to end the relationship and who gets what. "I love you until more pressing things than my death make it impossible to do so," would be a clearer promise. Could the reason for our reluctance to commit and opting for divorce be that the idea of staying in a relationship "until death do us part" seems un-doable in light of our increased life expectancies? In the first part of the twentieth century, the average age at marriage was twenty and life expectancy was about sixty. Today, the average person is married at twenty-five and, by 2011, is expected to live until about eighty. The difference is fifteen years of marriage.

Does the idea of spending the rest of our lives with the same person sound restrictive, when there are so many other people and goals to pursue in a lifetime? Is it no longer realistic to conceive of a love that lasts a lifetime? Our reasons for staying in a relationship or for getting married have drastically changed from those of previous generations. As we have become increasingly self-sufficient, economic security is no longer an incentive for marriage. Today, we seek gratification, romance, fulfillment, loyalty, commitment, and love!

Just as our reasons for entering into a relationship have changed, our success rate at staying together has declined. There is also a psychological reason why singles fit relationships within manageable time slots and remain aloof. With all the hype over what constitutes a desirable catch in the singles scene, many singles project an "on-top-of-the-world" image, as well as an "I-am-always-doing-great" attitude about themselves, both of which are very difficult to maintain in a close relationship.

Middle-aged and older singles often have developed an inflexible view of their lives and are apprehensive about the idea of another person intruding. Moreover, this group of singles is also restricted by their occupations, children, grandchildren, and aging parents who need their support. Frequently, the deteriorating health of older singles becomes a burden in a serious relationship. Today, many singles of all ages want to enjoy love without responsibility and interference in their daily lives.

❤ Road-kill on the Singles Superhighway

Even though single life is often being viewed as less restrictive than the boundaries of a relationship, most singles are definitely searching for lasting love. As it becomes more difficult to achieve this goal, singles turn to various dating services, which pop up in growing numbers with escalating memberships.

> *If I put a truckload of gravel in front of you*
> *and told you that there is a big diamond inside,*
> *would you ever quit shoveling?*
> — POPULAR SAYING

As they explore every conceivable avenue, the good, the bad, and the ugly surface everywhere. Some singles act as if they were shoveling snow in the middle of a major snowstorm and many become roadkill on the singles superhighway. An estimated 75 percent of all singles over the age of thirty have not had a date in the past year, and of those who did date only very few have encountered any long-term potential. With huge inventories of singles among the diverse love-finding avenues, each expects to find his or her peacock among the feather dusters.

I am old enough to remember weekend dates as a ritual. In an elevated mood, filled with great expectation, I would put on my most flattering outfit and, like a butterfly, float through the house before "his" arrival. In those days, my weekend dates created enough excitement to fill several pages of my diary and warranted a week's worth of chatter with my girlfriend. I am also young enough to have participated in what I call *Concealed Bathrobe Dating*. Curled up in my bathrobe, I sifted through singles profiles on the worldwide web and was excited to find all of them wired for sound. This dating revolution made a dress code unnecessary and I didn't even have to apply make-up before going online. My dating inventory received a huge boost from the allegedly hottest scrolling over my screen. Flattered by this enormous outpour of interest in me, I scrutinized faces and bodies with Netscape 3.1 or higher. My thoughts revolved around dot-com and dot-net and logging off began to feel as if someone had unplugged my life support machine. Occasionally, my cyber-chats turned into real telephone conversations and, sometimes, even into the prospect of an actual date.

Being too busy managing my numerous Internet relationships, I rarely had the opportunity to ever actually meet any of the *somebodies@somewhere.coms*. With this new technology telling me to log on, download, scan, insert, delete, and even spam, I felt equipped to search for even more perfect people in far-away places. Sold on the idea of a larger and diverse pool of singles with every keystroke, I saw a new beginning in every ending. Did I really believe I could accomplish via wires what I had not been able to do in person?

One of my friends romanced the world over, surfing the net until she latched onto a chap from "down under." The romance blossomed against the background of high-speed Internet access until it became obvious (if only to her) that heaven could not have made a better match than her omnipotent computer. Gearing up to raise emus with the man from the outback, she cashed in her life savings, sold her furniture, bought Australian Gold sunscreen and headed off into the unknown. Unhappily, upon arrival in Australia, she recognized that Mr. Outback was not the ideal mate she had envisaged. He turned out to be a heavy drinker whose life was in a state of chaos and he shared his apartment with an ex-girlfriend. My friend returned home asset-poor and wisdom-rich, but soon after, she found the love of her life in her own backyard, where it had always been patiently waiting for her.

Regardless of whether you met someone at a bar, via the Internet, through friends, or a dating service—the good, the bad, and the ugly are everywhere. There is still a lot of stereotyping at work regarding the whereabouts of the "good." Conceptions that losers go to bars and that the Internet is flooded with weirdos still partially guide the dating attitudes. Whatever method one uses to meet someone, no one method is better than another. In truth, the hit-and-miss approach is typical of any dating method, as is easily recognized in the following stories:

- ⇨ Shauna thought she couldn't go wrong if she trolled at the marina for a good-looking guy at the helm of a half-million-dollar yacht. She landed her goldfish and life seemed splendid until she realized that her "high-roller" was a psychopath who turned her life into a nightmare.
- ⇨ The minute Eleanor logged on to a singles website, she hit her windfall by finding real love with Bart, someone she would probably never have met without the invention of electronic romance.
- ⇨ Martin's life has blossomed during the many years of his marriage to Chandra, whom he had met at a local bar.
- ⇨ Kirk lined up with the "bitch from hell" at one of several blind dates arranged through well-meaning friends. This woman wrecked his car, went on a shopping spree with his credit cards and ultimately set his house on fire in a state of emotional rage.

I had so many blind dates,
I should get a free dog!
— WENDY LIEBMAN

The Internet makes it possible for people to be more deceiving about themselves, as was the case involving the gentleman whose wit encouraged my lengthy relationship with him via the "net." Unfortunately, even though his electronically stored photograph depicted someone in my age range, in reality he must have been considerably past retirement age, and unless I had immediate plans to become the widow of a wealthy man (which is what he claimed to be), he was not my destiny.

Internet courtiers who are deceptive to that degree live mostly far away from you and are usually not eager to meet you in person. Admittedly, personality deceptions and distorted background information are more common through e-mail exchanges. However, people are just as capable of hiding their true personalities in face-to-face encounters, and this presents a real challenge in discovering the core of the other person. In subsequent chapters, we will answer the burning question that everyone must eventually face: How do I know who the other person really is?

Through the partner-finding avenues available today, singles everywhere have come to believe that a large quantity of prospects provides greater chances of finding the diamond in the rough. While it is true that they might collide with their "one and only" on the dot-com superhighway to passion, they have just as much of a chance of downloading a project requiring considerable assembly. Notwithstanding the horror stories that you have heard about Internet romance, there are still serious singles who have logged on to ride the next wave of cyber-matrimony.

The Internet has become a growing social circle for singles of all ages and is flooded with self-promoting personal ads, which are often in need of a more truthful interpretation. Self-endorsements in full-scale ads can be as outrageous as the following, which generated a flood of inquiries:

THIS ONE WON'T LAST LONG!
Female: *Ageless (marinated in rejuvenating and age-defying products), passionate, drop-dead gorgeous bombshell ready to be indulged, looking for yet another ideal man to support my preservation. I am simply the best thing after sliced bread. (What was the best thing before sliced bread?) Did I mention that I am blonde? To apply for this position, please forward a complete resume with recent picture.*

Similarly, an ad placed by a male would generate numerous replies if it read as follows:

Male: *Very attractive, high-income-earning male, with a well-toned body and lots of time to spoil you. I am generous, kind, sensitive, caring, and a hopeless romantic.*

The response rate for these types of ads is high because they appeal to our fantasy of finding everything desirable wrapped up in a perfect package. Singles often grossly distort their images and personalities in order to compete against the huge number of ads in the marketplace. However, these singles will receive many useless replies simply because someone who replies to such an ad is looking for everything else but true love.

When we actually meet the folks who place such ads, a more truthful description would be:

Female: *Once gorgeous, but now rather wilted. I am an enthusiastic visitor of beauty and massage parlors, since my purpose in life is vanity. In my spare time, I like to shop 'til I drop. Only those with adequate assets and high, unexhausted credit limits need respond.*

Male: *Financially very much at ease due to inheritance. I possess no education or work history, as my sole occupation consisted of being a son. My sexual history is as mysterious as that of Bill Clinton. I have lots of potential, but am not motivated to do anything with it. My attitude will ensure a frustrating relationship. Only those who know how to admire a man need respond.*

❤ Internet Dating Services in a Nutshell

Internet dating sites allow you to connect both romantically and internationally. Sites such as *Single Again Online Magazine* or *Christian Café* organize members into categories. Ads accompanied by photos are said to generate the most responses. Fees vary among companies and often females are permitted to post ads at no cost. Most sites do not release your e-mail address to interested members without your permission. Singles Internet sites are either broad-scale sites with a large membership basis, or niche market sites, with diverse religious and non-religious spin-offs. Dynamic singles sites allow you to review members' profiles and provide unlimited interactive communication among members.

Many single sites have designed their business strategy for the long haul. They offer free trials to newcomers and respectable customer service. They make truthful claims and do what they humanly can to support you in your quest for love. Others, solely concerned with the short-term bottom line, skim funds from those seeking love while delivering little of what they promise. It is a well-known fact that the fast-growing singles market presents a perfect opportunity to loosen up substantial cash from the pockets of anticipative singles by selling illusion. As with everything else, it is a "buyers beware" scenario, and the onus is on the consumer to distinguish between the good and the bad.

❤ Matching Agencies

Matching agencies often operate like assembly lines and quite a few are disreputable businesses. Let me share with you a real-life experience from a not-so-reputable operation: A disreputable company claimed to cater to attractive and educated singles and, in doing so, it created the illusion of an inventory filled with the "cream of the crop." The advertisements featured handsome, sophisticated, and upbeat singles, alleged to have achieved lasting love through the company's proven method. The agency claimed to have a screening system in place to convince clients that only qualified singles were eligible. In truth, clients were harvested based on their ability to pay the outrageous fees for this highly questionable service. Like McDonald's slogan: "Over a billion customers served" (most undernourished), this particular company depicted attractive couples having found undying love without any effort. Nothing could have been further from the truth.

While the sheer number of available singles at these agencies evokes excitement, it distracts from the important human aspects of relationships and leads singles to be out of touch with reality. Their mindset becomes one of anticipating more perfect merchandise with each new referral, creating an inability to adequately explore another human. Dating and introduction services offer advantages for those who are shy, time-challenged, or lacking in opportunities to meet others. That covers just about everybody. However, I seriously question the business ethics of some companies that play with minds and hearts. While there are reputable dating agencies that are well positioned to assist in the search for a life partner, far too many companies fall seriously short in offering any valuable service.

One company has offered a system called *Speed Dating*. It advocates meeting about seven potential matches within an hour, and claims that it takes no longer than eight minutes to evaluate interest between parties. *Speed Dating* is based on the assumption that instant mutual attraction and love at first sight do happen. As much as we may fantasize about love at first sight, more often than not, love at first sight is actually lust at first sight. Moreover, research claims that 35 percent of love relationships commence because of love at first sight, but only 2 percent of those relationships last. Obviously, it does require more than luck, lust and chemistry to take a relationship from the initial excitement to building a meaningful history with another person.

With a whole host of partner-finding operations powered by either technology or reassuring human staff, many love seekers have come to believe that they never have to compromise in partner selections again. The choice as to who is the right partner can always be postponed, as a better catch might just be a keystroke or phone call away. Whether you seek a designer match, speed-date or Internet encounter, or whether you have your eyes on the local knock-out down the street, the safety principles and precautions for contact with a stranger apply universally. The chances of meeting your next spouse or a future stalker are the same for all partner-finding methods. Underneath all the fabulous, exciting personal ads and first-date impressions are humans with vulnerabilities who desire to be loved just like you and I. Even though many of the individuals you meet may not be right for you, most are basically good people. Most importantly, however, you must be ready to act upon love when it does strike.

While choosing the wrong partner is detrimental to your health and wealth, failing to take action with the right person can be equally destructive. Many people regret not having pursued the person for whom they felt love. While their reasons for not doing so are manifold, fear of rejection is predominant. This fear defeats more people (single or not) above anything else. Later in this book, I will explain the distinction between natural fears that protect us and fears that kill our desires and steal our dreams.

You may even belong to the group of singles who claim to enjoy the solo life. The majority of those praising this lifestyle are between the ages of twenty-five and fifty-four and are typically college or university educated. Those over forty date far less than any other age group. Many who worship flying solo actually experience emotional loneliness, and rationalize their lone lifestyle to a desirable level. Their reasons include having the freedom to do whatever they wish, spending their money on whatever they want, and not having to endure the flaws of another. The opportunity of dating whomever they want and not knowing with whom they might wake up in the morning often creates excitement for many veteran singles.

While there are no rights or wrongs, the rewards from sharing one's life and love far outweigh the so-called advantages of being single. The longer people remain single, the more inflexible they become about partner selection. One of the saddest consequences of increasing numbers of people opting for *singlism* is their desensitization to the family unit, one of the building blocks of our society. As a result, many singles contribute less financially, or otherwise, to their communities. A further consequence of *singlism* is a whole new generation of senior singles in the making, with a powerful impact to shift demographics and economics.

❤ The New Generation of Senior Singles

My friend Sue once sent me the following definitions of seniors:

- ⇨ My teeth and I no longer sleep together.
- ⇨ My health insurance is finally paying off.
- ⇨ I no longer need lifetime warranties.
- ⇨ There is nothing left to learn the hard way.

One joins the group of senior singles either by choice, through divorce, or upon death of a partner. Widowed senior singles often have little desire for a new relationship. Sometimes, they even feel they would betray their previous partner. Cherishing the memory of a lost love is often enough to live in contentment without further romantic involvement. Still, some senior singles are fortunate to find love again, but they are in the minority. Far more feel that they are over the hill without ever having been on top of a mountain. Seniors who are still in reasonably good health keep themselves busy with family, friends, pets, and hobbies. Most have gained qualities such as maturity, integrity, wisdom, patience, and life experience, all of which nurture equitable, harmonious, and rewarding relationships. Sadly, many of these seniors do not have such relationships and are missing both romantic love and sexual intimacy. Involuntarily single, they often live in despair questioning whether this is all life has to offer. This is particularly true of singles who have experienced divorce followed by a number of shattered relationships. Senior single life can be quite lonely, and many try to make the most of their abundant time while wishing for someone with whom to share their sunset years.

Being single at the senior stage is quite different than being single at a younger age. For younger singles, life still holds plenty of opportunities to find love. Younger singles often pay more attention to immediate concerns such as education, hobbies, and careers than they do to permanent partner choices. For aging singles who have not found the one they "don't want to live without," there is only limited time left to do so. For them, getting older often means that while they have gained an abundance of wisdom, their health is deteriorating and energy is decreasing. They often regret not having done what they wanted to do while they had the chance.

As the number of single households is increasing faster than any other, are we gearing up for a wave of senior singles even though most consider living alone undesirable? Research has long established that the well-being of adults is influenced by their social network, and more precise research shows that happiness depends on whether one has a confidant with whom to establish intimacy. While a confidant can indeed be someone other than a spouse, the healthiest and happiest people are those in loving, intimate relationships. To love and be loved is still the number-one desire of every human being, yet far too few people encounter real love. It is one thing to enter the senior years widowed with a history of a meaningful relationship but quite another to have never felt true love.

As a nurse caring for the terminally ill, my dear friend Beverly daily stares in the face of the dying, many of whom have not even entered their senior years. As she witnesses her patients' final moments of last reflection, she knows that their ultimate questions are: *Was I being loved and did I love?* Those who did not experience true love are dying in regret and despair, while those who did peacefully anticipate meeting their Creator. The meaning of life is not necessarily defined by the quantity of years that we live, but rather by the quality of love that we give and receive.

If it sounds like love, looks like love, feels like love, smells like love, and tastes like love it probably is love; seize it, for it may never strike again in your lifetime. If you are missing the deep love that you long for in your relationship, in most instances, you will be able to turn a present relationship around using the principles explained in this book. Stop thinking that you have all the time in the world to experience love and don't wait until your senior years, for love is all there ever will be. You are the author of your own biography, you always have been, and you always will be. If you haven't already done so, start writing your biography as a loving spirit, for you will not be given a chance to write a second draft.

❤ 5 Principles to Remember from Chapter One

1. You must stop being disrespectful towards your partner if he/she is not living up to your expectations.
2. You must respect your partner as you respect yourself.
3. You are always morally responsible to your partner.
4. You must throw your whole heart into your relationship.
5. There are no right or wrong places or faces for finding love.

Chapter 2

GARAGE SALE FOR SINGLES
The New, Used, and Abused

> *Lord, grant me the serenity to accept the things I cannot change, the courage to change the things I can, and the wisdom to hide the bodies of those people I had to walk over, because they really ticked me off.*
> —Author Unknown

NOT ALL SINGLES are created equal. Those most in demand appear to conform to society's standards of attractiveness, physical appearance, intelligence and financial security. These so-called perfect singles float around with ample social skills and consider themselves emotionally healthy and stable. They can fool almost everyone. Often when you meet these singles who appear as having everything "figured out," you become acutely aware of your own shortcomings.

Even though singles do the best they can with what they know, *singlism* (or off-and-on *singlism*) often leads to emotional detachment. Unlike those in fulfilling relationships, singles experiencing multiple relationships generate an abundance of memories but fail to produce any significant history with one person. As such, their sense of belonging rarely stretches beyond the gym or golf club.

The *Used, New* and *Abused* singles use defense mechanisms to survive in the highly confusing world of singles. Defense mechanisms create the illusion of control over their lives and shield their vulnerabilities. If singles desire a life beyond survival, control and defense, here is their "wake-up call": *It is time to realize that a life shared is a life truly lived.* While their single life can be exciting and fulfilling, much of their most rewarding human capacity: to love and be loved, remains untapped. Consequently, too many singles become dogs that no longer bark. The following categorization of singles is intended to take a serious, but kind, look at them. I hope you remain open-minded and non-judgmental while encouraging singles to be themselves.

After hundreds of interviews conducted for this book, it became clear to me that all singles are looking for unconditional love, regardless of how disillusioned they have become. If you are among them and are still asking whether unconditional love exists, you need to know that the answer begins with you. You must learn to give what you expect to receive. If this appears a hopeless proposition beyond your imagination, you might want to reclaim the perceived glory of single life and forego reading the rest of this book. If you choose to retreat, I ask you to pass this book to a single friend so that another dog may learn to bark again. On the other hand, if you choose to continue in your quest for unconditional love, this chapter is for you! Know that it will be up to you to help change the way singles relate to each other and remember that if you raise Hell long enough, Heaven will eventually listen.

❤ The New

These *New* Singles enter the scene freshly out of broken relationships. Ready to start a new and promising life, they invest in a new haircut, makeover and wardrobe. They have read the self-help books, signed up at the local fitness club and did it all (and more) at the speed of lightning. Their enthusiasm is contagious.

When asked what went wrong in their past relationships, they answer: "It just didn't work," and add with conviction that they are "over it." They are quick to point out how adventurous single life is (and it can be), and that they are now ready to explore their full potential and opportunities. They re-assure you that they are not searching for another "relationship" just a "friend." Great, you could use a sane friend who holds the secret to being emotionally healthy.

Soon you begin to admire this new-found friend, whom I will call Irony, for all the books he has read, his knowledge, his tennis trophies, his commitment to a toned body and his dog, the influential people with whom he socializes, his taste, his freedom and good spirits. Before too long, you notice that something is missing in Irony: compassion for the human race. Irony is into himself "head-over-heels." His appointment book bristles with self-indulgence, but only those who admire him are among his friends. Ironically, he only has time for you if you listen to him psychoanalyze his previous relationship (and you thought he was over it!). Irony has become emotionally disconnected from those around him. He sees himself superior to the rest of the world, engages increasingly in intellectual activities, and is obviously not over his past relationship. He has not really learned to love anyone but himself. Do you still think he is emotionally healthy?

❤ The Used

Used singles could also be called *seasoned* singles. Having been single for many years with a number of relationships "under their belts," these singles have become accustomed to single life and the regime of ending relationships. Most of the *Used* singles could have written parts of this book. These singles have the ability to spot another single from afar, as they are always looking for something or someone—yet are not sure for what or for whom. Each time they are given an opportunity, they tell a very different story about their hopes and expectations. Their likes and dislikes change depending on the listener (someone who sparks their interest, though it may only be for one night).

You can very easily identify the *Used* by their uninvolved presence. Although they may be newly available in the singles world again, they are certainly not new to the game. They will complain that there aren't any decent singles of either sex around and tell you that they have more-or-less given up on ever finding love, *except* if the "right person comes along."

The *Used* are quick to fill you in on all their accomplishments and the faults of their numerous past partners. This conversation almost invariably includes a past partner who still loves them and wants them back. If you are a *Used* single yourself, you will agree with another *Used*, and before you know it, there are two almost perfect singles surrounded by imperfect singles. The *Used* single is your ticket to eternal single life and he/she will forever try to convince you that most singles are not worth the time of day.

❤ The Abused

The *Abused* Singles are stuck in the pain of the past with no hope of relief in the future. They have been used, taken advantage of, taken to the cleaners and feel "hard done-by." When they lost their money, they lost a lot. When they lost their friends they lost even more, but when they lost their faith, they lost everything. They tell you all the details about how their former partners undermined them and you start feeling sorry for them. They present themselves as total goodness, incapable of even using insect spray and your heart opens up. They recite chants such as, "I did everything for her/him and was betrayed." "I raised her children from a previous marriage, while she screwed around." "I helped him become rich, but he used me as a doormat."

These singles are always the victims of either someone else or some unfortunate circumstances, and they are always powerless. Should you fall in love with an *Abused*, understand that you will pay the penalty for what others have allegedly done to him or her. They evoke sympathy from others and confuse sympathy with love. They are comfortable in their role as victim because they receive what they desperately seek: sympathy and attention. Are they beyond repair? Not at all, but they may be more than you can handle. Relationships with *Abused* are definitely not emotionally healthy!

❤ Who Stopped the Payment on Our Reality Check

While few singles fall precisely into any of the above categories, the classifications can be helpful in recognizing some behavior patterns. By no means am I suggesting that singles in these categories are losers. It simply means that many are like puppets, held together with strings that keep them together today but may rip apart tomorrow. In truth, most of us (including myself) have some weak strings and loose ends.

The "Emotionally Healthy Person" as defined by society through a wealth of contradictory "How To/Not To" publications may be forever in the making. While some of these guidebooks help us improve, many make us feel flawed and inadequate. Psychiatry has long focused on what is wrong with us and how to fix it. Obviously, some of us are better handymen than others, but with all this knowledge and awareness there are more depressed and unhappy people in our society than at any other time. Why is this the case? I suggest that someone stopped the payment on our reality check by convincing us to strive for perfection. Many of our attempts to transform into perfect beings start with identifying our imperfect or negative qualities. This focus on the negative merely contributes to our feeling inferior. (Later, I will discuss this in more detail to confirm that you are, by all odds, perfectly normal.)

Throughout our lives we are taught what to think, how to behave, which values to accept and what to strive for. In other words, if we simply eliminate undesirable elements in ourselves and replace them with socially desirable traits, we will lead lives of perfection, success and happiness. Most have accepted this paradigm like obedient sheep, but this is not the only choice in our pursuit of happiness. Instead, we ought to focus on the positive and that which is right within us, acknowledging that there is more right with us than there is wrong. Recognizing our strengths and positive qualities enhances all of our life experiences, contributes tremendously to our well-being and, most importantly, allows us to flourish as human beings. It is our birthright to experience happiness, joy, and fulfillment. Above all, we are meant to experience love.

❤ The Emotionally Healthy Person

The psychologist Maslow listed the following characteristics to identify an emotionally healthy person (Jourard, 1974):

1. They see reality, and knowing "the facts are friendly," they accept reality more than most people. They see through phoniness, deception, and "games"—and avoid them. They cope with problems, rather than avoid them.

2. They accept themselves and others; thus, they can honestly self-disclose and forgive others' shortcomings.

3. They are spontaneous with their ideas, feelings, and actions, being genuine and confident.

4. They focus on solving problems but their "problems" tend to be outside themselves. For instance, they often have a "mission" that may be difficult to accomplish but gives excitement, challenge, and purpose to their lives.

5. They enjoy privacy, withdrawing sometimes to be free to have their own thoughts. Occasionally, they may have mystical experiences in which they become part of all mankind or of nature.

6. They resist culturally prescribed roles, e.g. masculine or feminine. They resent unfairness caused by social roles and prejudice. They insist on thinking for themselves and completing their mission, even in the face of social criticism.

7. They enjoy and appreciate the commonplace, the little things in life—a rose, a baby, an idea, a considerate comment, a meal, a loving touch, etc.

8. They feel a kinship, a closeness, a warmth, a concern for every human being.

9. They are close to a few people, although not always popular. They can live intimately and love.

10. They do not judge others on the basis of stereotypes, like sex, age, race, or religion, but rather as individuals.

11. They have a strong self-generated code of ethics—a sense of right and wrong. Their values may not be conventional but they do guide their lives.

12. They are creative and do things differently, not in rebellion but for the joy of being original and talented. They are clever, even in their ability to be amused instead of angered by human foibles.

Unfortunately only about 1% of the total population displays *all* of the above traits. Guess what? You probably don't belong to this elite group and neither do I. Since the remaining 99% of the population displays up to half of these characteristics, most of us are a long way from being entirely emotionally healthy as defined by the experts.

The issue of emotional health is a hot topic for most of us and we have been bombarded with blueprints of how we should be. Some of us have even put parts of our lives on hold in anticipation of reaching the state of emotional well-being. We continue our search for emotional health, because we have been told repeatedly that true love only comes to those who have no baggage, scars or hang-ups. Nothing could be further from the truth. The idea of reaching this ultimate state is a utopian illusion.

We all have emotional imperfections and that is why most of us still cry over spilt milk. This was the case for Susie Homemaker who did not let herself fall in love with a wonderful man. In a guilt-ridden state, she had decided that raising her children was more important than her relationship with him. Today, this wonderful man has become a loving, understanding and supportive life partner to another woman, who considered him just as important as her children.

Love comes to those who believe in love, regardless of the circumstances. But society has turned us into fault finding machines and we feel pushed to the limit. We have become experts in finding fault in ourselves, in our circumstances and in others. Fault finding and focusing on the negative has separated and alienated many of us. Instead, we should permit ourselves to be who we are and to discover the goodness in all of us. In my view, self-actualization means getting to know who you are and being proud of it. A pat on the back is much more productive than a stab in the back, and that holds true for all human beings.

To realize that nobody is perfect is one thing; to accept this fact in ourselves and in others is quite another. It takes an open and courageous heart to love the imperfections in us as well as in others. By the end of this book you may find that you have what it takes to move beyond and to become who you ought to be. You may find that while you are looking for the diamond in the rough, you have come to a gravel pit full of polished diamonds with yourself among them.

In the June, 2000, issue of *Psychology Today*, Martin Seligman Ph.D., former president of the American Psychological Association, was called "The Freud of the Next Century." Here are some of Seligman's views on psychology's shifting focus to the positive:

> *"The overall goal of 'positive psychology' is to enhance our experiences of love, work and play. This is a revelation for a group (psychologists) that has focused on dysfunction, illness, healing and coping strategies. It is no surprise that in the psychological literature over the last 30 years, there have been 54,040 abstracts containing the word 'depression,' 41,416 naming 'anxiety,' but only 415 mentioning 'joy.'"*

Seligman believes that only a small number of the 18 million people diagnosed with depression actually suffer from biologically based depression, which, according to him means that our conception of depression is all wrong. Maybe, "What looks like a symptom of depression—negative thinking—is itself the disease," says Seligman.

It is very encouraging to know that Prof. Seligman is at the crest of the next wave of psychology, "Positive Psychology," on an academic and professional level. I have long believed that people have collectively made themselves mentally and emotionally ill and that the entire world in which we live reflects this attitude. It is no surprise that an increasing number of unhappy people can do no better than shape an unhappy world with a decaying environment.

❤ Someone's Garbage Becomes Somebody Else's Treasure

The exciting beginning and devastating end of a relationship is a familiar paradox for most singles. They have "been there, done that and bought the T-shirt" which says: *New, Used, Abused and Single*! (If you pick up the business idea of making these T-shirts, please make them bullet-proof.)

All our relationships begin with excitement and high expectations. Each time we believe it will be different because we are convinced we have learned so much from previous relationships. At some point the learning needs to stop and we must do the right thing. Getting it right, however, means living with gratitude in the present, rather than in the past or future.

The initial stages of our new relationships are marked by elevated endorphins, pheromones and heartfelt chemistry. Eventually, however, relationships kept afloat by these chemicals start sinking.

During my years of counseling I have seen Titanics sink and Bridges of Madison County collapse for all the same reasons. After the newness of the relationship wears off, you begin to spot faults where you saw perfection, flaws where there was beauty and stormy waters where there was smooth sailing. You are left staring at your unfulfilled hopes and reach the point of disillusionment. You degrade and blame each other for everything and anything, turning each other into garbage until one of three things happen:

1. You dump the person.
2. You are dumped.
3. Both of you open up your souls and show your precious selves.

Unfortunately, the third alternative rarely happens. More often the dumping of garbage takes place and, in order to justify another failed relationship, you declare the other person a liar, jerk, bitch, plain stupid or otherwise not good enough. Some of you write off the relationship as just another learning experience, without ever asking, how much longer you want to continue the lesson? You attempt to learn other skills with the goal of mastering them. Yet, when faced with learning life's most gratifying skill, that of loving, you call it quits before the lecture is over. Ironically, the garbage you dump eventually becomes someone else's treasure. You observe this jerk, bitch, liar, etc., happily melted into the arms of another, just after you have put him or her through the compactor. This piece of trash suddenly looks better, seems happier and whether you like it or not, this person has "risen above."

At the beginning of a relationship we are programmed to impress and seek approval for who we are. Research has repeatedly proven that people use more energy to impress strangers than they do to impress family members and friends. The reason for this is that family and friends already know us, making it impossible to conceal our faults and flaws. As long as strangers, co-workers and acquaintances do not become our close friends, we are able to selectively portray positive impressions of ourselves. We behave in this way out of our need to be liked and appreciated and out of fear that our true self is not lovable. As we get closer in relationships, it becomes difficult to maintain the impressions we have projected and even more difficult to continue to act the part. Through relationship after relationship we think we have become more knowledgeable about what we, as well as others, want in relationships. We have dating tips coming out of our ears and, if still in doubt, enlist a psychic. We have given our lives away to the experts when all we really need to do is be ourselves. *We can never be truly loved for who we pretend to be.*

When the true *self* of the other person becomes apparent in a relationship it almost invariably spells disaster. We feel somewhat betrayed and misled because he or she concealed their true self. Too often, we tend to dismiss the relationship without questioning whether these uncovered flaws and faults are really as disturbing as they appear.

Take the case of Jean Watchdog, who set herself up for disappointment by looking for Joe's faults. After a few dinner dates with Joe and having received flowers on each occasion, he invited her to his home. He was out of toilet paper, a disaster by her standards, and needless to say, he did not keep the toilet seat down either. There were no flowers upon her arrival and the cleanliness of his house reflected that of a man who works long and hard hours every day. Jean retreated from the relationship, claiming his shortcomings unacceptable and refused to see that those little things did not matter at all. In so doing, she never discovered the kind, loving and sensitive soul of Joe. Jean watched for the bad signs and missed the good ones. Someone else saw them. She bought the toilet paper and taught Joe to leave the seat down.

In hundreds of my counseling sessions (I prefer to call them re-focusing sessions), I encountered singles that regretted having prematurely ended relationships long before they ever really got to know the person (more about why relationships end prematurely in following chapters). All the advice on how to recognize the wrong partner like a weed in your lawn can sometimes be very misleading. One should not lose sight of the fact that most people are good people and what appears to be a weed is often a flower waiting to be discovered. Still, I recommend staying away from the irresponsible, seriously mentally disoriented, drug dealers, child abusers, pathological liars, etc.

❤ 5 Principles to Remember from Chapter Two

1. All singles do the best they can with what they know at the time.
2. A life shared is a life truly lived.
3. You have to learn to give what you expect to receive.
   "Do unto others as you would have them do unto you."
4. There is more right with all of us than there is wrong.
5. Most of us are not totally emotionally healthy and that is normal.

Chapter 3

ARE WOMEN FROM UTOPIA AND MEN FROM WAL-MART?
Physical Differences vs. Human Commonalities

Our gene pool could use a little chlorine.
—Author Unknown

THIS CHAPTER IS DEDICATED to all women and men interested in discovering the human commonalities between the sexes that are numerically more significant than their differences. These commonalities may come as a surprise considering how many writers, psychologists, and scientists have made it their life's work focusing on these differences. While I appreciate the efforts of those who have documented these differences to help men and women understand each other better, I believe that men and women are much more alike than the world cares to admit.

In our male-dominated society it is no coincidence that men have undertaken the bulk of the work revealing these differences. Historically, the sexes have been assigned rigid gender roles and men and women have adopted these roles more-or-less faithfully. The goal was, and in many ways still is, for one of the sexes to emerge superior and more adapted in this dog-eat-dog world. When Charles Darwin published his book, *The Origin of the Species* (later *mis*interpreted as "Survival of the Fittest"), he never suggested that males were superior or more adaptable than females.

Traditionally viewed as the inferior sex, women felt compelled to assume utopian attributes such as nurturing to the extreme of self-destruction, giving to the point of running on empty, and self-denial in favor of their families and the expectations of society. As a result women have been accused of being overly emotional, unrealistic and capable of little more than shaving their legs or operating a vacuum cleaner. In contrast, the "superior" male sex has been praised for its Wal-Mart attributes of being realistic, practical, efficient and intelligent. Consequently, men run the country, hold most of the assets and control the majority of public and economic affairs.

❤ The Physical Division of the Blues and the Pinks

Even a brief review of history suggests that our gender roles have been arbitrarily assigned. During World War II, the US government recruited women for factory jobs vacated by a male population gone to war. Suddenly, these fragile, weak and inferior women operated heavy machinery, manufactured munitions and built bombs and ships as adeptly as they had run their sewing machines and assembled sandwiches. To make my point, when the country was at stake, women were persuaded by the men in power to perform jobs traditionally occupied by men. After the men returned from war, they reclaimed their jobs; and women were forced out of the labor force, and sent back home to care for their children and husbands. Encouraged by images of sexually available, nurturing and childbearing females, women have been expected to be slim, pretty and, ultimately, user-friendly.

Even though much has changed since then, we still embrace society's standards of masculine and feminine traits to a large degree. We have even accepted that feminine traits, such as being nurturing, are biologically based, a belief heavily promoted by a male-dominated scientific community. Ironically, scientific opinion once held that the earth was flat!

While we change our beliefs either in the light of new evidence or if our old beliefs no longer serve us, we have historically clung to beliefs endorsed by public consensus. Our style of thinking is that if everyone believes that all swans are white, it must be so. Our tendency to think in generalized terms continues until someone discovers a black swan. Today, most of us believe that men and women are significantly different in every respect. Does clinging to this belief really serve both sexes or even encourage their growth and unification on a human level? I firmly believe that the focus on our differences has served to divide us instead of bringing us closer together.

The obvious physical gender differences, such as our sex organs, are reason enough to celebrate our differences as they are intended not merely to continue the human species, but to give and receive love. The fact that boys have historically worn blue and girls have worn pink is nothing but a societal norm of gender division. So much time, effort and money has been spent (and made) on exaggerating emotional, intellectual, hormonal and communicative differences between men and women that we indeed believe ourselves to be from *different planets*. I urge you to look beyond the differences and discover that women cannot live without Wal-Mart, nor can men live without utopia. Women need Wal-Mart for the practical, logical and task-oriented aspects of their lives and, in fact, may be shopping at Wal-Mart more often than men. On the other hand, men need utopia to experience all the beauty and humanity of life, and are visiting utopia more frequently than they would ever care to admit. We are all from the same planet. It is about time we bridged the gap between the sexes and realized that we are simply human beings with many of the same needs, desires, dreams and hopes.

Whatever the case may have been in hunting-and-gathering societies of the past, today we are all hunting for the same things and gathering the same goods. Men and women alike are hunting for love, happiness, validation and prosperity, and are gathering whatever they feel is necessary to achieve this. Now, more than at any other time, men and women need each other in the pursuit of these common goals.

❤ Society Has Played a Trick on Us

Society has imposed a rigid code of gender socialization and we have been brainwashed from early childhood to believe that the feelings and experiences of men and women are dissimilar. Specific behavior and feelings are either encouraged or discouraged according to gender. While much has changed, we still live governed by rules that prescribe different behavior and activity for men and women. In many ways, inferiority has to a varying degree been attributed to women and superiority to men. Traditionally, women have been grouped with the weak and inferior. Indeed it has been common thinking to rescue women and children first along with the blind, deaf or otherwise challenged. It wasn't until the 20th century that women in the United States were allowed to vote and it took even longer until they were allowed to say no to sex in their marriages. The majority of Americans still have a preference for sons, particularly when it comes to their first-born. Many parents still encourage or discourage feminine and masculine traits in their sons and daughters, which creates a very different frame of reference for children of both sexes.

I am not suggesting that women should be viewed as superior or become more liberated than men. Instead, I simply recommend critical examination of our beliefs concerning gender differences. Do you really believe that investing in gender stereotyping will encourage men and women to become best friends and lovers? The truth is that loving relationships form when both have moved beyond their gender differences and respect and love each other because of their human commonalities. Are satisfying love lives the result of catering to each other's different sex needs? No, rewarding love lives are based on the realization that men's and women's bodies are both designed to enjoy making love when they feel respect, love and trust in a relationship. Men and women do not stay in love because they have spent every moment trying to figure out their differences. Instead their love grows and matures as they allow the human potential in each other to flourish. Lovers do not feel connected and united because they have learned everything there is to know about men and women. They evolve together into free human beings allowing each other to interact without judgments.

This brings me to the "F-word": feminism. Most people harbor conflicting thoughts about feminists, and with many contradicting versions of feminism in circulation today, it is no surprise that we are not sure what to think. Perhaps, it is easier to dismiss feminism altogether as it has a radical ring for most of us.

The work of the faculty in Women's Studies at the University of Western Ontario has opened my eyes to the fact that human commonalities in both men and women are what allow us to relate to and understand each other. Contrary to popular belief, feminists are generally not the bunch who asked, when we sent a man to the moon, "Why did we not send them all?"

Feminism has made us aware that women are to some degree still being undermined and treated unequally. It has helped us to understand that the victim does not encourage physical violence and rape. While feminism continues to strive for safer streets and homes for wives, mothers, daughters, sisters, aunts and girlfriends, women still feel safer walking the streets at night in the company of a man.

Yes, women can open all the doors themselves, but they still appreciate a man extending this courtesy. They can create a life of their own, financially support themselves and even do oil changes or file their own income tax returns. Women can shop for the best Wal-Mart bargain and also splurge on Godiva chocolates. They can raise their children to become fairly decent adults. They cry over a romantic movie and get a thrill from the *X-Files*. Women become jealous of the Victoria's Secret models and develop lusty thoughts when they spot George Clooney or Russell Crowe. They are touched at the sight of puppies and babies who represent life, but are outraged at violence, which dishonors life. When making love they like to be "on top" as well, and be responsible for their own fulfillment. Women can be independent when they need to be and dependent when they want to be. They prefer to share their lives with a man because they choose to, not because they feel they have to.

Most women no longer burden men by making them responsible for their partner's happiness. Women want to be in solid relationships, be loved and respected as human beings. We need to free each other from the gender roles that society has cast upon us and start focusing on the ties that bind us.

❤ The Menstruating Pilot and the Male Mother

Not so long ago, society demanded that women stay home and raise children. In those days, the quantity of time a mother spent with her children was a priority. The widely held belief that women are less intelligent, somewhat unreasonable and emotionally erratic supported their confinement to the roles of mother and housewife. In more recent times it became apparent that a single income earner was insufficient to maintain a comfortable lifestyle and consume all that is available. As women entered the workforce, they were stuck in lower paying, lower status jobs because of their lack of education and job skills. Society quickly shifted its emphasis from spending *quantity* time with children to spending *quality* time. Women were expected to perform their duties as mothers and housewives as well as work at their newly acquired jobs.

To add to their burden, women were expected to stay slim, sexy, attractive, loving, caring and emotionally balanced. In their attempts to meet these expectations, many women lost their identities, values, self-worth, beliefs, spirits and even their minds.

> *My wife has a devoted husband, a beautiful home, two healthy children, a part-time job, a gym membership and enough money to buy anything she wants. But she is miserable, moody, and does not appreciate how hard I work to afford her this lifestyle.*
> —COMMENT OF ONE OF MY CLIENTS

The typical doctor's diagnosis for a woman having difficulties coping with the life designed for her by society is that she most likely suffers from PMS. With many women struggling to meet the expectations of their families, employers and society, PMS became an officially recognized disease not only for physical symptoms but also for women's psychological anxieties. Prescription drug sales skyrocketed as the answer to women's silent revolt. Women were declared unsuited for the positions of pilots or any other jobs carrying tremendous responsibility because of monthly emotional hurricanes. Women's frustrations and inabilities to live up to the Superwoman image were dismissed as PMS symptoms.

While there are real PMS symptoms due, in part, to hormonal changes, much of the so-called PMS symptoms are exaggerations and are really due to the stress in the lives of women. For pharmaceutical companies PMS is a true gold mine on which they are cashing in, "big time." For most women, however, popping pills does little to solve the root problem.

On the other hand, men experience their own stress in a competitive world that still expects them to be the pillar of their families. Not too long ago, men were considered incapable of nurturing and even forgiven if they were incompetent fathers. Men were programmed to be the sole provider of economic security in the nuclear family and understandably experienced their own anxieties. Feeling the pressure of maintaining an affluent lifestyle or even just making ends meet, they became workaholics, grew bellies, lost their hair and became candidates for heart attacks. This pattern still continues.

Women's stress is documented in association with the psychological symptoms of PMS. Men's stress is linked to physiological illnesses such as heart problems, and men commit suicide five times more often than women. Both men and women experience stress trying to become Super-humans in a society in which they feel they never quite "cut it."

Preoccupation with the differences between the sexes has often prevented men and women from asking each other for help. Consequently, we have suffered silently through our own pain and blamed each other for our differences and lack of understanding: "Men are never this" and "Women are always that." As a result of the generalization of our differences, men "shut down" and women retreated to their therapists (often falling in love with them). The era of divorce ensued, followed by the division of kids, homes, dogs, other assets and, not insignificantly, hearts.

Baby boomers made history in the name of self-fulfillment,

becoming the ambassadors of this new *"me-first"* society. For most, the expected liberation through divorce did not happen. Instead, they found themselves with broken hearts and shaky economic futures. Many justified the painful events of divorce by claiming to be finally free from the former spouse who had turned their life into misery.

Divorce makes us wonder whether men failed women, or *vice versa*. While men and women were trying to meet the expectations arising out of their respective gender roles, they did not realize that both suffered equally. As a result, men and women failed each other. Men and women were indeed living as if they were from different planets and did not connect intimately as human beings.

Gender differences have been analyzed to death, and you may never be able to understand a man or woman by the definitions of scientists and other disciples of these differences. However, you will always be able to understand and respect a human being once you realize that all of us are human beings first and men or women second. Inside each of us, men and women alike, lies a vulnerable soul, the desire to love and be loved, the need to be validated, respected and to feel important. While counseling singles and couples, I realized that, regardless of gender, deep down we all have a fragile ego that often feels inferior. Recognizing that both sexes have many of the same vulnerabilities and strengths is the key to men and women relating to one another on a human level.

❤ The Opposite Sex Is No Mystery

As women are gaining more independence, liberation and equal opportunities we see a role-reversal of men and women. More men are dealing with dirty diapers, shopping for groceries, doing housework, trucking children to and from activities and helping with homework. More women than ever before are hunting for their independence and validation as complete human beings, changing tires and mastering remote-controls along the way. We find more men and women watching soul-touching movies and real life events with heartfelt emotions. While men still go to the barber and women to the beauty salon, it appears that for the first time they are blending the worlds of utopia and Wal-Mart. More men than ever are finding their inner capacity to nurture and care and have become emotionally available without embarrassment. They are freeing themselves from society's macho standard and are displaying soulful behavior. Many Baby Boomer men have lost much through divorce, experienced financial setbacks and even lost their jobs. The ever-increasing demands of their workplaces or the fear of failing businesses have made them realize that they, too, are vulnerable and not always in control.

Men's liberation lies in being allowed to be human and free to ask for support from women. Men are beginning to value women as true friends rather than competitors. Fortunately, their well-intended role as protector and provider seems to be evolving to a new level.

We do not need a separate dictionary tailored for males and females to understand each other. Nor do we need to elaborate on our possible or impossible differences. We do not need to visit other planets to discover the hidden secrets of men and women because *there are no secrets*. Men have learned much about the right romantic gift but, more importantly, men and women have learned that the need to be connected to each other is central to their lives. This fact makes us more similar than not.

In his book, *Men Are From Mars and Women Are From Venus,* author John Gray advances a number of theories concerning the differences between men and women. In the second chapter, he suggests that a woman's sense of self is defined through her feelings and the quality of her relationships and goes on to state that on Venus, loving relationships are more important than work and technology. Being a woman myself and having interviewed hundreds of women, I have formed a different opinion. I believe that a woman's sense of *self* is defined by how much she is permitted to use her full human potential. Today, women have assumed the roles of astronauts, police officers, doctors, senators, CEOs of high-tech companies and tough-litigating lawyers. Women have become activists against violence, child abuse and drunk driving and proponents of human and animal rights. In doing so, they pour their whole hearts into their causes. For many women their sense of *self* is defined by their accomplishments and the ability to make a difference in the world. While a meaningful relationship is still essential to women and is part of the definition of the *self,* it is not the sole purpose of their lives. Today, almost as many women as men are discovering that careers and self-actualization have become important aspects of their lives. Even though many women appear to indulge in their newfound independence, the truth is that they, too, are seeking the interdependence of a relationship in which they can be, and become, all that they are.

Men's desire to be *free* and women's right to be *upset* is another example of the differences between the sexes given in John Gray's book. He states that men need space while women need understanding. In asking many women about their key issues, I discovered that the desire to be free is just as paramount for women as it is for men. Women want the freedom to pursue their own purpose in life and be liberated from many of society's unreasonable demands. They want to be free to spend their days in jogging pants (however un-sexy) and to "dress to kill" whenever they choose. They do not want to be judged by the cleanliness of their homes or how well they keep themselves in shape. The right to be upset is not the issue for women. The real issue is the right to be accepted for all that they are. Like men, women appreciate space and time to themselves, allowing a chance to "become centered." Men and women alike need mutual understanding and respect as they face life's stresses and demands.

Instead of suffering and coping on different planets, men and women are realizing that they experience the same fears, anxieties, insecurities and challenges. The commonalities between men and women are so much greater than our differences. As we change our attitudes towards each other, we will be able to relate better to one another on common ground.

The notion that lasting love between opposite sexes is only possible when we appreciate that our focus on gender differences has been of great disservice. For any relationship to become a stable and lasting anchor in our lives, we must learn to give up our pride and our unrealistic expectations of each other. If you are hoping to find true love in this misunderstood world of males and females, I encourage you to stop trying to figure out the opposite gender (some things you will never understand). Instead, keep reading this book and learn why it is essential to regard and respect each other as human beings in all your relationships.

❤ 5 Principles to Remember from Chapter Three

1. Men and women are from the same planet with many of the same needs, desires, dreams and hopes.
2. Men and women need to free each other from the roles cast upon them and start focusing on the ties that bind them.
3. PMS most accurately translates into "Positive Money Source."
4. Attitudes and beliefs about the opposite sex are socialized and do not necessarily reflect the truth.
5. Men and women need each other more than ever.

CHAPTER 4

DRIVING SCHOOL FOR SINGLES
Park, Reverse and Drive

> *Watch for big problems,
> sometimes they disguise
> great opportunity.*
> —Author Unknown

IN CHAPTER 2, in somewhat exaggerated terms, I described three broad categories of singles: *New, Used* and *Abused*. Many of you have undoubtedly identified with a particular category or have at least begun to similarly categorize other singles. In your quest for love you have certainly met many singles and may have observed that some remain motionless and unresponsive. In fact, you will observe that quite a few are as inflexible as railway tracks, refusing to bend for life's curves (although they are pliant for specific curves). Regardless of where you are in your journey, take comfort in the fact that in every journey there is meaning; in every conflict there is growth; in every action there is purpose, and in every moment of doubt, remember to believe in yourself.

While searching for the answer to their loneliness, many singles display specific learned behaviors that are indicators of their progression. Too often, they have stared in the face of love but chickened out. For many the fear of rejection and their inability to surrender to love outweighs their desire to capture love.

Singles commonly reach states akin to positions on a gearshift: *Park*, *Reverse* or *Drive*. In these states, they send conflicting messages about their identities, making it a small wonder that many are confused or discouraged by their peers. Often they seek pseudo-psychiatric therapy from each other but rarely shift into *Drive*. Too frequently they dabble in the tricks of love rather than focusing on its skills. In a sad attempt to attract one another, some may leave the inertia of *Park* to spin their tires in a cloud of rubber, while others remain stuck in *Park* or *Reverse*.

I sincerely hope that this chapter will inspire "single readers" to encounter more meaningful and loving experiences. In the end, they may shift from *Park* or *Reverse* into *Drive* to become like a Ferrari: best in full acceleration, with the driver in charge!

❤ Stuck in Park and Reverse

Stuck in *Park*, Kathryn makes a grand entrance at the local bar. Like a peacock, feathers unfurled, she glides over her imaginary red carpet. Cinderella has arrived at the ball ready to receive the admiration of all. After all, she has coiffed, sculpted and primed herself for two hours. Her preparations involved an even longer dress rehearsal so that she might ascend to the throne like a prom queen. Now, her sole reason is to count the number of men whose heads turn to gaze upon her and hopefully line up at her sleeve. At the end of the evening she spends as much time de-fluffing as she has in her preparations. Kathryn repeats this ritual *ad nauseam*. While she may lose some fake nails and lashes in the process, she has yet to meet a real suitor.

Although Kathryn desires love in her life, she remains alone in front of her make-up mirror lamenting her empty heart. She has created an image of herself as untouchable, unapproachable and unattainable. Beneath her facade is a frightened woman trying desperately to compensate for her insecurities. At some point in her life she bought into the idea that love must be earned, and that glamour and attractiveness were required. Consequently Kathryn believes she cannot be loved purely for who she is. She will continue to conceal her true self and strut her stuff until the final curtain. Why does she expect different results when she does the same things over and over?

While the exaggerated example of Kathryn depicts a soap opera image that is not representative of the average single, it nevertheless reminds us how far we often go to conceal our insecurities and seek attention. Society has taught the Kathryns of this world that being lovable requires nothing more than being attractive and in demand. No wonder we encounter, to a lesser extent, many such Kathryns preening themselves and fabricating their appearances in the image of sought-after love-objects. Instead of humanizing their souls, they are defining their marketability like any other commodity.

Sir Lancelot is another embellished example of a single stuck in *Park*. Taking to heart the advice to "Float like a butterfly but sting like a bee," this clean-cut social butterfly enters the scene with a winning smile to survey the crowd. As soon as all heads have turned his way, Lancelot jumps into action. Like a bumblebee, hovering from bloom to bloom, he stops for a few moments to engage each woman in idle chatter, unconcerned with anyone in particular. Still, he asks himself why he has not found someone who really loves him. Many women refuse to become involved with the likes of this drone, since he is unconcerned with their intellect or other qualities. Lancelot sends a message that he is indiscriminate about the company he keeps, and that he seeks encounters without substance. It is no surprise that he is commonly repelled.

Sir Lancelot masquerades behind an armor of calculated behavior to disguise his true feelings of inferiority, and to mask his fear of intimacy. Eventually his emptiness and the lack of involvement in a heart-felt relationship will yield a hollow echo. Lancelot, in search of someone to respect and love, is trapped in *Park* and buzzes from woman to woman. In truth, he may never be able to take on a queen bee.

Stalled in *Reverse,* Miss Retro, a throwback to the 60s, lives a major part of her life in the mind-set and attire of days gone-by. Her wardrobe reflects items retrieved from mysterious places out of the past and her hair style proclaims that not all hair dresser from the 60s have retired. She evaluates all relationships by astrological signs, yet fails to recognize that the singles' super-highway is covered with Stop and Yield signs.

Miss Retro is often attracted to younger men who generally cannot identify with her era. She may not grasp in which part of the 60s she is stuck, but maybe it was in the 60s that she last felt happy. Miss Retro will continue to convey mixed messages until she realizes that she is out-of-sync, and makes a conscious choice to live in the present.

These exaggerated examples of singles trapped in *Park* or *Reverse* are an indication that for most, the fear of loss is greater than the desire for gain. Kathryn's fear of dropping her mask overpowers her true desire for growth and intimacy with another spirit. Like all other Kathryns, she is susceptible to all who shower her with attention and consequently is left blinded and unable to appreciate another. Sir Lancelot's fear of losing moments of glory in the social limelight is greater than his desire to bond with anyone on an intimate level. Miss Retro has chosen to hide in the familiarity of yesterdays because her fear of leaving the past is greater than her desire to embrace today.

The gears of *Park* and *Reverse* are simply states or coping techniques employed by those who fear true love and intimacy.

Often they fear they are not good enough or not lovable enough, and generally do not trust others. Moreover, they are not even aware that their behavior teaches others how to treat them. Surprisingly, almost all singles believe that loving would be so easy if only the right person came along.

As demonstrated in the previous examples, singles stuck in *Park* or *Reverse* seem to be more concerned with the superficiality of being admired and sought-after than sharing the platform with another human. In order to experience the richness of giving and receiving love, they need to shift from *Park* or *Reverse* into *Drive*. *Reverse* is a state many singles enter either after a relationship failure or if the prospect of a new one appears hopeless. A state of *Reverse* also exists when singles review past relationships with bitterness and are unable to forgive those who have hurt them. Other times *Reverse* means regret over allowing a former relationship to fail without having given it one's all. Singles in *Reverse* also become progressively more withdrawn in order to protect their precious hearts from further pain.

The positive aspect of *Reverse* lies in the opportunity for self-reflection and subsequent healing. Reflecting on one's life and accepting responsibility for the failure of past relationships can be very productive. Another constructive aspect of *Reverse* is that of identifying who you are, what you want and what you believe in. Some singles shorten this *Reverse* stage by recognizing that even though they did the best they could, they must do things differently to get different results. Eventually, these singles finally realize that life rewards action, not passivity, and shift into *Drive*. They give their lives new direction by attaining higher education, learning new skills, taking up new hobbies or becoming physically fit. They simply develop into better people by making different choices and, in the process, find new friends and even true love. Unfortunately, not all singles use the state of *Reverse* productively, and many allow valuable years to slip by without ever changing gears.

Many somewhat bitter singles have lost their faith in a brighter future and live in a state of emotional detachment. Having voluntarily settled into loneliness, they often grow bored with themselves and consequently have little to offer others.

Another familiar scenario of singles stuck in *Park* and *Reverse* is the "your couch or mine" style of pseudo-psychiatry. *Parkers* or *Reversers* act out reciprocal roles of psychiatrist and patient. Having met by choice or chance, two strangers pour out the intimate details of their latest relationship disaster. Their totally predictable dialogue is a paradigm of one-up-manship for the most wounded heart but, no matter how stellar the performance, no Oscars are awarded. After a lengthy session of former-partner bashing, the newfound pair feels sufficiently connected at the soul to recline the couch to a horizontal position.

Submission to the illusion of inexpensive "your couch or mine" therapy bears the hidden cost of soul erosion. In reality, the pair are donating their bodies (with fragile souls attached) to sex therapy, believing themselves to have latched onto someone who cares. This Dr. Fraud scenario simply provides chicken feed for the soul. There isn't a human soul in this world that can flourish on chicken feed. These *Parkers* and *Reversers* drive aimlessly around the parking lot without ever finding the exit.

❤ Permanent Singlism

Apart from singles who have consciously chosen to remain alone, there are many who are completely unaware that their attitudes and behavior guide them on a direct path to permanent *singlism*. These permanent singles have unwittingly created a barrier that makes them appear aloof and unapproachable.

Their mind-sets send clear messages to others that they are not interested in a relationship, yet in their hearts they feel quite the opposite. As a single, you may recognize yourself in this category or, at the very least, identify some of your single friends with characteristics typical of permanent singles.

A number of years ago, I spent a lot of time with a friend whose permanent *singlism* became the cause of her loneliness. When I first met Karen (who I hope and pray reads this book) I was taken aback by her carefree attitude, intelligence, mastery over her life and her impeccable appearance. She seemed to have it all together and managed what appeared to be a life by design. My own attempts to develop a carefree attitude and easy-going lifestyle were constantly interrupted by my personal responsibilities and unpredictable life events. My action-packed life seemed more like a roller coaster next to Karen's predictable, organized and mainly uneventful life. My time was always challenged and self-indulgent moments were rare. I envied Karen for her abundance of time until I realized that much of her free time was spent in loneliness or with meaningless tasks. Her immaculate hair styles made my head look as if I always had bad hair days. Her outfits represented an art of well-studied color and style coordination, prompting me to question my own appearance. Making plans with Karen was a real chore requiring at least two days' advance notice. She had no room in her life for spontaneity and needed everything to work according to her plans.

Karen had other annoying character traits, even though she was otherwise very likeable. When she suffered from a simple headache, Karen suspected a brain tumor or at the very least a neurological pathway acutely damaged. On days when her mood was not as elevated as she liked it to be, she diagnosed herself with anything from severe depression to bi-polar disease.

Her forgetfulness was rooted in either Attention Deficit Disorder, or worse, a premature onset of Alzheimer's disease.

Karen followed a disciplined diet and her nutritional needs became the center of our conversation. I began to feel guilty over even looking at a French fry. She nursed her diet, aches, pains and mood swings excessively, simply because apart from her 9 to 5 job she only had herself to think about. Even her most minute problems required world attention and soon I realized that our conversations revolved solely around her interests and concerns. I noticed that whenever I talked about my life, she brushed me off with a drop-dead example out of her life. Simply put, I never had an opportunity to share my ideas, problems, dreams, hopes or fears with Karen. Finally, I came to the conclusion that she was only interested in me as an audience, not as a person. Karen loved to take the spotlight and listen to herself talk. My own life was very different from hers. I did not have the time or inclination to blow my own minor problems or aches out of proportion. I was passionately involved in the lives of those I loved, cared for and who depended on me. I cherished those meaningful relationships. Karen had lost this passion for others a long time ago and instead reinvested it in herself. I wondered if she had read too much about the joy of being single and had taken the advice of "loving yourself" too far.

Karen was distinctly different from those who are simply single. She was completely absorbed with herself and had developed a "permanently single" mind-set. Unfortunately, the older she became and the longer she lived on her own, the more she sunk into herself and wondered why she was still single. Ironically, she blamed her loneliness on the inability of other singles to open up to a relationship. In truth, Karen had no place in her life, her heart, her soul or her mind for anyone but herself. Every moment in her life was occupied with self-absorption and anyone wanting to get close to her was shut out. She no longer knew how to include another person in her life on an intimate level.

There are many singles of both sexes unaware that they are just like Karen. Some soul-searching would be in order to identify the attitudes and behavior that may contribute to permanent *singlism*. Being wrapped up in purely self-absorbing thoughts is guaranteed to keep any interested party at a distance. The *first* step out of this trap is to admit when you are in it.

The *second* step is to realize that you have chosen to become self-centered and in so doing have opted for the consequences of still being single. Even if you try to convince yourself that it is not your fault that you are still single, the fact is, you are! You alone have the power to change by changing your thoughts and behavior.

The *third* step is to recognize that others are just as important and valuable as you. To actually escape this cycle of permanent singlism, you must open your heart to others and begin to care again. Like everyone else, you too have a natural ability to consider, care for and nurture others if you choose to do so. However, if you are in denial about being in a state of permanent *singlism*, you may never be able to escape it.

Singles who are caught in the unproductive conditions of *Reverse* or *Park* are committing the biggest crime of all: failing to live in the present. As they avoid the risks of involvement, rejection and failure, they sabotage their happiness.

If you find yourself in *Reverse*, it may be time to cut the ties that bind you to the past. Your time in this life is not negotiable and every moment counts. All the knowledge and insight you have gained about moving into action are worthless unless you shift into *Drive*. At the end of your life, I will guarantee that you become painfully aware of everything you didn't do and didn't feel, including love.

Parkers are very similar to those in *Reverse*. The key difference is that *Parkers* are not clinging to the past. *Parkers* perceive themselves to be living in the present but they are spectators of life, not active participants. These singles are fearful of going anywhere where they have not been before. Their lives are wish lists of dreams, expectations and things to do. Often their lives are filled with monotonous activities that provide little excitement or happiness. Even though they are unhappy about how their lives have unfolded, they accept just about anything life dishes out and feel powerless to initiate change.

Parkers have not entirely given up hope and believe that what they desire in life will occur someday down the road, just not now. They suppose that love will strike them out of nowhere, perhaps when their children have grown up, when work projects become less demanding, when clients stop calling, when they are financially established or when they have lost weight, just not today. Someday they will travel to Rome, watch *Gone with the Wind,* read Hemingway, eat healthfully, exercise and watch a sunset, volunteer at the food bank, support a child in need or rescue a puppy. Someday they will live near the ocean or on a mountaintop, help the old lady next door and even fight for a cause. Someday they will experience true love, actually hear when they listen, share their lives (or what is left of them) with another person and someday they will give without expecting anything in return, just not right now.

Now, there are more important things to do. Meeting deadlines, keeping the house clean, scheduling their children's activities, updating their wardrobe, installing the latest software, keeping up with soap operas, accessing more information than they know what to do with.

They may have big plans for someday, but unfortunately someday does not exist in their day planners and for these

Parkers someday means when it is possibly too late. When it is too late, *Parkers* have one more excuse. At least they have had every intention to live more, love more and share more. They have had every intention to live life with awareness, love, joy and happiness but never got there. Even though they are aware that time is running out, they are unaware that there will be no "rain-checks."

Parkers live in anticipation of what might be in store for them, but they put the best years of their lives on hold. In doing so, they miss many opportunities; however, these opportunities are never truly lost, because someone else will seize them. *Parkers* believe they have to pay their dues now in order to later have love and happiness.

> *There once was a snail and it lived in its shell*
> *and then it died.*
> —BEVERLY WILKINS

While *Parkers* hold the vision of someday attaining a state of happiness and love, their mindset prevents them from moving beyond intentions.

We have all listened to the truisms: "Life does not reward intentions, only actions," "You get out of life what you put into it," "You create your own reality by your own thoughts and emotions," "You are always responsible for your own life." We hardly require the daily news to be reminded of our mortality. Our lives can end in countless ways: cancer, car accidents, murder, heart attacks, diseases, parasites, plane crashes, wars, storms, volcanoes, floods, fires and terrorist attacks. Wake-up! *Carpe diem*! Seize the day for it may be your last. Why do these messages not sink in?

From the *Parker's* perspective, remaining in *Park* is safe.

There is no risk of fender benders, running out of gas, ignition failure or head-on collision. If you find yourself unable to shift out of *Park*, don't blame yourself. Instead, continue to read this book and you may become inspired to make some changes and to test drive the Ferrari you are meant to be.

> LIFE AT RISK
> *To laugh is to risk appearing a fool*
> *To weep is to risk appearing sentimental*
> *To reach out for another is to risk involvement*
> *To expose feelings is to risk exposing your true self*
> *To place your ideas in front of a crowd is to risk their loss*
> *To love is to risk not being loved in return*
> *To live is to risk dying*
> *To hope is to risk despair*
> *To try is to risk failure*
> *The greatest risk in life is to never risk anything at all*
> —Author Unknown

❤ Drive

Drive means moving from the immobile state of *Park* or *Reverse* to engaging all your senses completely in the flow of life. It means filling up with gas (permitting only positive beliefs to enter your mind), rotating the wheels (shifting your attitude), placing your foot on the accelerator (refocus from intentions into actions) and, most significantly, heading in a direction of love and happiness.

Singles in *Drive* have awakened from their former sleepwalk through life and are geared up to move out of *Park*. They only use *Reverse* to remind them of where they have gone astray. These singles have tapped into their tremendous capacity to love and their ability to become happy. These underused capacities are accessible to each of us.

Singles moving into *Drive* have learned much from their pain and know that they can only grow from a loving heart. They have dispelled the beliefs that confined them in *Park* or *Reverse* and stopped blaming themselves and others for past mistakes. They have realized that blaming themselves only undermines their self-worth and confidence. They have ceased fulfilling the expectations of others, have expanded their own potential and have changed their attitude about themselves and others.

As singles in *Drive* focus on the positive characteristics and the decency within them, their authentic spirits emerge. They no longer compare themselves to others. They let go of their fears of the future, release their judgments and grow tolerant and respectful of the differences in others. As a result, they develop *emotional intelligence*. Many restore their faith in true love and become emotionally available, while others make the decision to cherish the freedom of being single until they feel prepared for love. In any case, singles in *Drive* become clear about who they are and leave little room for assumptions and misrepresentation about themselves. They have learned to contribute love to every moment and live richer lives.

❤ Learning the "Trade of Love" Instead of the "Tricks"

In Chapter 2, I suggested that we often put more effort into impressing strangers than acquaintances. Most of us wear an assortment of masks as we play our various social roles. For example, a police officer may play the roles of father, husband, brother, son and soccer coach. For each role, he wears a different mask and it is not surprising that he encounters role conflicts. In the case of singles, they are taking their dating roles and identities to new, dizzying heights. Many single women outfit themselves with the latest seduction devices in their battle for a date with an equally mistaken belief system. Men on the other hand are known to have gone as far as renting a Porsche for a date, while being delinquent in child support payments. Consequently many singles exhaust a great deal of time and money to become social magnets. No longer is it sufficient to make a favorable impression or sweep the date off his/her feet, the individual must be knocked flat on his/her face or even committed to the intensive care unit!

Using an abundance of advice on how to attract love, many singles interchange their identities to adjust to their current dates. They maintain a high degree of conformity with the current standards of dress codes, behavior and political correctness. In this process their efforts are spent on landing dates instead of seeking love.

To find love you must stop looking for love in push-up bras, in wallets, or in superficially acquired behavior. If you are to capture true love, you must reveal who you are and what you feel. You must wear what you favor, be who you are and disclose what you believe in. *Only your true soul can ever be loved or surrender to love.* No matter how deeply you buy into the tips and tricks on how to amaze the other, tricks only produce balloons of illusion and relationships doomed for failure. The sooner you end the charade of "do's" and "don'ts," the closer you will get to what you are trying to find.

The point is that it does not matter what you are or are not, because neither is good or bad. What matters is that you live and behave in accordance with who you are. In doing so you will attract someone who accepts and loves your true self.

*We are all in the gutter, but some of us are
looking at the stars.*
— Oscar Wilde

❤ 5 Principles to Remember from Chapter Four

1. The fear of loss is often greater than the desire for gain.
2. The Now is all you have and tomorrow never arrives.
3. Opportunities are never lost. Someone else will seize them.
4. Intentions are meaningless unless they are transformed into actions.
5. Really living is to know what love is.

CHAPTER 5

LOOKING OVER THE SHOULDER
Commitment until something better comes along

*If you think the grass is greener on the other side
maybe it is time to fertilize your own lawn?*
—Author Unknown

THE PREVIOUS CHAPTER described how singles prime themselves for failure in love. It portrayed how singles assume a "dating identity" and head off to yet another date, hopeful that this time they will stumble upon a candidate who meets their expectations. Although this may be possible, concealment of their true characters and pursuit of illusive expectations almost invariably steer them down the path of deception. On this off-track journey, they accumulate never-to-be-redeemed Air Miles ™ and the love they seek remains out of reach.

A careful survey of this planet demonstrates a transformation almost everywhere, but perhaps no clearer example can be found than in the aftermath of the September 11, 2001 attack on the World Trade Center. More than at any other time, we have witnessed acts of love and kindness: people risking their lives to rescue others, passion in assisting the less fortunate and going the extra mile towards making a loving difference.

While our political views on the causes of the attack may vary as much as our individual interpretations of the U.S. response, there can be little doubt that around the world people are uniting in the spirit of love and exercising a collective influence. Every time the seed of love is being planted through loving acts toward humankind we see triumph emerge. Yet, far too few of us are sowing these seeds. Like so many, you may have a gloomy and dispiriting global vision. However, after reading this book you will have gained insight into the transforming power of love and it will be entirely up to you to use it. You yourself are like a seed and ought to prosper in love where you have been planted. This book aspires to restore your confidence in love and to inspire you with abundant material to fertilize your boundless capacity to love and be loved. It is your choice to blossom or wilt.

Regardless of how many fruitless relationships you have racked up, and no matter how discouraging your present relationship may be, you are in the company of millions. Just like most, you are contemplating the meaning of relationships either while in a liaison, just out of a relationship or about to launch a brand new one. If single, you may harbor serious doubts about the splendor of single life and may sense emptiness.

Off-and-on singles believe that they began their relationships for the right reasons and in the right way. All of these relationships ended with common reactions such as, "Next time I will be more aloof," "Next time I will care less, love less and guard my heart with barbed wire." These reactions only serve to minimize one's capacity to love and to make one more judgmental of others.

Those who take action instead of just reacting to relationship failure accept responsibility for the break-up. Instead of finding fault only with their former partners, they also examine how they failed their partners. No matter how much they have been hurt, they are able to forgive and forget by acknowledging their hand in the rift.

Interviews with singles revealed that what they say and do is inconsistent. While the majority of singles claim to seek a soul mate, their actions reveal very different intentions. Unless the soul mysteriously slipped below the waistline (or waste line) it is obvious that today much dating occurs between the sheets and that the soul is not the guiding principle. The apparent motives for entering into a relationship are attraction to another individual, the need for physical contact and companionship. While these reasons fulfill innate human longings, they will not necessarily foster honest, empowering and intimate relationships.

This chapter provides insight as to why many of us encounter multiple disappointing relationships that lack direction, assurance and commitment. It explains why we stay, why we leave and why even apparently committed lovers gaze over each other's shoulders to a nearby stranger.

❤ I Love You Because I Don't Know You

Typically, when we fall in love we do so with someone whom we hardly know. Mesmerized by the fantasy of love, more often than not we pursue love for its own sake. Indeed it is the power of this fantasy that prematurely pushes us into full-fledged relationships as we ignore our gut feelings and forebodings of trouble. Love is, however, neither blind nor deceptive. More precisely, we are blind. Our deep desire to be loved distorts our senses and blocks our view of the other person's moral fiber. It is so easy to love a person we don't know, and even more enticing to be in love with the imagination of our minds.

Not only do we play-act for each other, we also invent visual and mental illusions of one another. Well into the relationship we may begin to wonder, "Was he always this hairy?", "Did she always have that gap between her teeth?" "Was he always this self-centered?" "Was she always a drama queen?" The resounding answer is "Yes." Having disregarded our internal hunches we now turn into fault-finding machines. "Love is blind" really means that we have chosen to see only what we want to see and are blind to everything else.

When a relationship deteriorates each party exaggerates the other's imperfections and blames the other. At this point, some may terminate the relationship while others continue to look over their partner's shoulder until a better somebody comes along. This is a complete betrayal and even though these individuals are not single yet, they rationalize a single status because they feel dissatisfied with their current relationship. Seduced by superficial excitement or a need to supplement missing elements in their present relationship, many persistently scan their surroundings for targets of affection. Many justify their taste for forbidden fruit (affairs) by simply finding fault with their present partner. However, it is mostly lack of intimacy and the hope of finding intimacy and acceptance with someone else that prompts this over-the-shoulder activity. Ironically, failure to build intimacy in the present relationship is a definite indicator that intimacy in a subsequent relationship will not develop.

Intimacy is not a disposition found in another person. More accurately, it is a bond shaped by two willing people that intensifies over time. Failure to create this bond in relationships, leads to emotional and physical withdrawal and ultimately to growing resentment. In looking back, many have experienced one or more relationships in which the resentment grew faster than kindness and support for each other. As a matter of fact, this is exactly what happens when relationships take a turn for the worse and the person we thought we loved becomes the reason for our frustration. The predominant communication style consists of blame and defensiveness while holding the other responsible for the problem and expecting him or her to provide the solution. Instead of creating the best possible relationship, we use our energy to facilitate deterioration. Relationships only cross the threshold to love when we become *fit to love* and, in so doing, learn to respect and be morally responsible to each other.

At least 50 percent of singles I have interviewed have been in relationships in which one of the parties looked over the other's shoulder. More than half of these better-than-nothing relationships (BTNs) ended because one partner became involved with another person (claimed to have found someone better). This phenomenon is accompanied by distinct conduct. While many favor monogamy in their presumably faithful BTNs, they most certainly are not mentally monogamous as their minds and eyes marvel at other prospects. People justify being in BTNs because of fear of sexually transmitted diseases, fear of loneliness, the need to be loved and not wanting to let go, just in case someone better does not come along (hence the term BTN).

Mr. Scanner and Ms. Grateful have been in a relationship for over a year. Ms. Grateful has enduring faith that this relationship will be her final one and therefore values this union. It satisfies her need to be wanted, offers companionship and permits her to build "castles in the sky." Little does she know that Mr. Scanner regularly surveys the scene for available females. Even though he appreciates Ms. Grateful, he has not allowed himself to truly love her. He feels something crucial is missing in their relationship, but, unable to identify the issue at heart, he opts for unproductive solutions elsewhere. His observable traits are typical of the over-the-shoulder type: lack of commitment, inability to listen, lack of passion and absent-mindedness. Regardless of the type of relationship, these symptoms are a definite signal to open up communication. But Ms. Grateful and Mr. Scanner are both in denial. Ms. Grateful persists in her attempts to stimulate a close bond between them, forever compensating for the absence of honesty and intimacy. No matter what she does, Ms. Grateful cannot make Mr. Scanner fall in love with her. All she can do is stalk him and hope he will give in. While she is astute enough to believe in undying love, unless both of them recall the positives that attracted them to each other in the first place, everlasting love will not emerge. They will remain emotionally unavailable to each other, making it impossible to resolve conflict or address each other's needs. Apparently Mr. Scanner and Ms. Grateful entered into this relationship for the same reason: they are more interested in being loved than they are in loving.

This holds equally true for Ms. Want-It-All and Mr. Name-Your-Price. Their relationship arose from infatuation. Beautiful, young and dependent Ms. Want-It-All thought she "struck oil" when she met this man who had it all. Their attraction was mutually superficial and while her beauty, youth and neediness mesmerized him, she was fascinated with the prospect of a lifetime of affluence and comfort. Mr. Name-Your-Price named his price: she had to maintain her beauty and youthfulness so that he could inflate his ego by parading her around. In return, Ms. Want-It-All jetted to the most luxurious destinations, went from beauty parlor to fitness clubs, to diet centers, to golf courses, to noteworthy events and shopping malls. Along the way she acquired a stunning wardrobe, designer jewelry, cars, stocks and bonds, life insurance and prominent friends. Concealed beneath her extensive inventory is a damaged soul. Having lavished all his wealth upon her, Mr. Name-Your-Price needs her only to hang like a trophy on his arm. In the meantime, Mr. Name-Your-Price has preserved the spotlight and is convinced that hard currency is the strongest tie that binds. Ms. Want-It-All insisted that money was a great substitute for intimacy as long as there was lots of it (and if there was a *will*, she wanted to be in it). Mr.

Name-Your-Price continued to pay the price, growing ever aware that her devotion was only gratitude for benefits received and that his feeling for her was that of pride. Clearly they mutually satisfy each other's superficial needs, but over the course of their relationship they were plagued by truth-seeking questions: "Would I be the object of his admiration if I weren't attractive?" "Would she have chosen to be with me if I weren't rich?"

As their respective desires to be loved remain unfulfilled, she resents her magnificent captivity, her dependency and the manner in which she sacrificed her identity. He exercises even further control and manipulation over her because he derives his power by disempowering her. In the end, the spurious desires that first ignited their relationship will continue to bind them. However, as their desire for true intimacy resurfaces, they will look over each other's shoulders to seemingly greener pastures.

Beginning a relationship based on superficial reasons does not always have to spell disaster. However, the reason for an unsuccessful relationship can often be traced back to how it started. In simple terms, when you begin a relationship for the wrong reasons, those reasons will remain the underlying factor for its termination.

❤ Cover Me, I Am Changing Lanes

You may have recognized yourself or your present or previous partner as an over-the-shoulder type. This awareness might keep you guessing where these relationships are leading or if they are leading anywhere at all. In this section we will look at those relationships that come to an end because one partner becomes involved with someone else and is about to change lanes. In these instances, one of the partners develops an infatuation for another person that swells into a full-fledged affair. The current partner may be unaware of obvious signals for a pending lane change but in almost every case, the precursor of the affair and the ensuing end of the relationship are evident. Nearly everyone is familiar with the obvious cues: new haircut, starting to work out, late hours, new wardrobe, new hobbies, etc. This behavior can be ambiguous, since it may also be found in anyone embarking on a path of self-improvement. Still, there are some less obvious signs found in partners changing lanes and here is the rationale for them:

- Cheerless in your company: they assume you suffer less if a miserable person departs.
- Find more faults in you than ever before: they want to validate their lane change.
- Find fault with your friends, relatives and approach to life: they need to convince themselves that it would never have worked.
- Avoid relationship debates: they are afraid of lying even more.
- Avoid going down memory lane: they want to retain as few memories as possible.
- Steer clear of conversation about the future: you might not be part of their future.
- Decline physical contact whenever possible: they feel as if they are betraying their new lover.
- Put off making decisions: they may not be present when the decisions become effective.
- Only discuss issues one day at a time: they may hit the road the next day.
- Wear "Do not disturb signs" on their foreheads: they occupy a different world.

⇨ Avoid romantic movies with happy endings: they prefer movies that portray survivors of failed relationships.
⇨ Check their e-mail frequently and rigidly delete, dump and bury it: they do not want to share their fresh relationships with you.
⇨ Contact with their friends intensifies noticeably: they need them as back up.

As lane-changers approach their new liaisons and receive sufficient reassurance, they invariably feel buoyed to chart a new course. They enlist support from friends and relatives by strategically criticizing their former partners and complaining about incompatibilities. As soon as the road is paved, over-the-shoulder types are ready to change lanes without hesitation. Their current partners are typically offered a rehearsed explanation in all too common terminology, such as: "We were not destined to be together," "You wanted more than I could give," or "We are simply incompatible."

After this relationship has officially ended, with the endorsement of family and friends, lane-changers head for greener grass. In truth, they have failed to fertilize their own lawn while the opportunity was there and now the grass on the other side requires even more fertilizer. The outcome is fairly standard in the new relationship that has emerged against a background of distrust and deception. New partners should therefore not be surprised when the lane-changer repeats the cycle of over-the-shoulder behavior.

❤ The Human Spirit Can Never Commit to a Compromise

Over-the-shoulder and lane-changing relationships are examples of compromising relationships that focus on the missing elements of both partners. As a consequence of ending these relationships, the separating partners will typically drift from one relationship into another. Singles over the age of 30 have, on average, 3.7 relationships (lasting 3 months or more) during a 7-year period.

Evidently, countless *Used, New, Abused, Parkers* and *Reversers* pass through parking lots in search of love. Many become involved in a relationship while looking over each other's shoulders. Others simply pull out of relationships that they are no longer prepared to endure. Regardless of the explanation, there are a lot of beginnings and endings over the course of a typical person's life and even more lust, fondness, infatuation, passion and obsession.

The term "love" is misapplied to most of these scenarios but only a small number will ever discover "the real thing." In nearly all of these "in-and-out" relationships we observe two strangers working out their quandary of loneliness and need for physical closeness while remaining indecipherable at heart. After they have exposed and drained each other, they recognize that their contrived nearness has nothing to do with love. Then, they pursue new relationships with the optimism that their longing for true love will be satisfied. The majority of these individuals are not conscious of this self-deceit. There are critical failures routing people through numerous relationships and into continuous deception:

- ⇨ Failing to disclose to each other the uniqueness and depth of their relevant personalities.
- ⇨ Believing that love is a sensation arising early in a relationship with another person.
- ⇨ Being programmed to stereotype women and men.

Every time we set a new relationship in motion, we do so according to assumptions about what makes us desirable to our new partner. Even though we fabricate momentary illusions of love, these are only passing chapters in our lives. The attitude that love is a gooey feeling emerging if the right person turns up, rather than an act of one's free will, explains the confused connections of many.

In revealing interviews, countless people expressed regret that some of their fleeting relationships did not advance to the height of real love. They also commonly confessed that their lane change did not take them to greener pastures. As a consequence, many lost trust in love, have misguided judgments about love and create emotional barriers. Most importantly, they are not *fit to love*. Fortunately, most of us have still not given up hope that we will someday stare in the face of love. Hopefully, those who have read this book will change their outlook and safely travel along the road towards a loving relationship.

Never steal hope, for it may be all we have.
—Author Unknown

Hope is supported by acquired, sustained beliefs and human desires. If the beliefs about love are false, the desire for love will escort us repeatedly onboard sinking ships. These misguided beliefs about love need to be reconsidered in order for us to become *fit to love*.

❤ Choose Your Love and Love Your Choice

Many relationships with the potential for true love fail because of finger pointing, avoiding conflict resolution and lack of commitment. However, while these and countless other reasons may be cited for the breakups, the underlying factors are always lack of *mutual respect* and *moral responsibility*.

To understand *mutual respect* and *moral responsibility* we must first tap into our humble, authentic self. Without finding our authentic self we cannot know who we are or what we want and are therefore unable to love and respect another person. Instead of dealing with the authentic self, we continue to play roles and remain victims of the needs and expectations of others. If these roles are not in alignment with our true self, we create disharmony within and are incapable of opening our hearts and souls in the face of love.

The authentic self embodies the truth about us, and without this courageous truth, love and intimacy will not blossom. There is something amazing about this truth. It liberates us to be who we truly are and fosters harmony within. Since the authentic self is the gateway to love and happiness it really needs to be distinguished from the role-playing, performing self.

The distinction here is quite down-to-earth. The authentic self encompasses truthfulness, respect and dignity in every circumstance while the role-playing self aspires to be anything from Wonder Woman to Mr. Know-It-All. The authentic self masters the art of self-knowledge. It does not conceal character traits, and it avoids misrepresentation. The authentic self is your precious autonomous self that focuses on your talents, abilities and honorable qualities. It is not distressed by self-doubt or feelings of inferiority. Most importantly, the authentic self has no desire to play games with the mind of another.

We are all born with the knowledge of our authentic self, but we lose this connection early in childhood. As explained by Barry Neil Kaufman in *Happiness Is a Choice* (p. 186–188):

Little people are forever busy, their endless motion unencumbered by judgments and self-incriminations. They are the planet's great adventurers, genuine explorers who dare to bring themselves fully to every experience. They don't simply go with the flow; they are their own flow. They don't simply act happily; they are happiness in action.

Very young children are forever authentically themselves; they do not experience the internal dissonance and short circuits of role-playing in accordance with external standards. They take their cues from within. We recognize their innocence immediately as a precious commodity. Their uncensored presentness beguiles and intrigues us and, perhaps, becomes one of the major reasons we want to help and protect them.

When a child goes from person to person or activity to activity, the same little creature presents himself or herself in each circumstance. No protective masks are used, no roles modeled and no extra clothing worn to camouflage or impress others. Children naturally display a wholeness of person without study or premeditation.

Most of us view those first years as sacred and blessed. And yet they do not endure. Rather than encourage such innocence, delight and enthusiasm, we quickly introduce cultural standards for everyone to follow. Perhaps in our childhood, our parents or guardians may have celebrated us for precious weeks, month or even years. They may have encouraged us to explore our fantasies and develop our imagination in a world of playful explorations. But then, inevitably, the agenda

> *changed. For our own protection, those around us said we had to learn how to act, what to say and what to want. We became little belief consumers, internalizing notions of good and bad, right and wrong, should and should not. No one distinguished between prejudice and objective data. No one separated myth from facts. We internalized it all, mostly without question.*

How do we unlock the authentic self in adulthood? We can start by disposing of the opinions and convictions that bind and confine us. In the process, we become aware that much of what we do or say is not in alignment with who we are. While our attitudes and beliefs are subjective, our hearts never lead us astray. The authentic self acknowledges and communicates its feelings and beliefs regardless of what is considered acceptable.

Many of us, and particularly the over-the-shoulder types, have not always acted honorably in relationships and have yet to encounter our principled relationship *persona*. Consequently, we are exceedingly suspicious of one another on issues of love, commitment, responsibility, integrity and intimacy.

If you are among the suspicious or have not always conducted yourself honorably, do not abandon hope. You can still discover your true self at any moment and begin to trust your capacity to love and be loved.

While you can never make a better past, however undignified it may have been, your past does not determine your future. You can choose to become a loving, dignified and honest person. By the end of this book you will realize that everything you need to embrace a life of love, self-respect and integrity is within the exceptional person that you are. In fact, you will be able to salute your authentic self with liberation and confidence, if you so choose.

When you maintain a relationship while looking over-the-shoulder you commit mental or physical infidelity and consequently lose both dignity and integrity. At some point, when you eventually stare in the face of true love, you will have a track record of undignified relationships.

If you finally choose love you will need to cultivate a virtuous character right now. This is possible, regardless of how you have conducted yourself in the past.

Character calls forth character.
—JOHANN WOLFGANG GOETHE

Rationalization of emotional or physical infidelity in over-the-shoulder relationships is a denial of the authentic self, as it involves misrepresentation of oneself and irresponsibility towards another human. Over-the-shoulder relationships in which individuals deplete each other psychologically and spiritually to the point of physical illnesses are generally beyond repair.

Conversely, relationships that have not reached this sad state still have the potential of becoming gratifying. Unhappily too often, we avoid problem solving at the start of these relationships and later on opt to either change lanes or end our relationships. As the storm mounts and waves rise, we watch our ships sink instead of reaching for life jackets. In the end, promising relationships now turn into over-the-shoulder situations or end unnecessarily.

Those who wish to discover true love in their relationships will have to disclose their innermost selves, since no one can get the "love thing" straight otherwise. Suppressing feelings and vulnerabilities conceals our most loving and compassionate human qualities.

> *Love is the extremely difficult realization that someone other than oneself is real.*
> —Iris Murdoch

As we discern our true self and begin to trust ourselves, we become aware of the reality that others are just as real and capable of loving as we are. We make ourselves lovable by being loving and we learn to trust by trusting ourselves.

Far too many of us are apprehensive about love and the fear of being hurt keeps us stagnating. Most of us modify our identities in relationships to gain approval, to be loved, to acquire fame or fortune, or to satisfy diverse other requirements. At the onset of new relationships we are anxious to have our needs met and consequently we keep score. We invariably measure the likely success of our relationships by how satisfactorily our wishes are being fulfilled. We miss the point that true love has no strings attached and does not keep score.

As a result of misguided beliefs about love, most relationships never achieve real love. Instead, the outcomes are rootless relationships that are subject to uncertainty, misinterpretation and much speculation.

In summary, the main reasons why relationships with the potential for intimacy and true love turn into sinking ships are as follows:

- ⇨ Failure to expose one's true self.
- ⇨ Unrealistic expectations.
- ⇨ Failure to foster friendship.
- ⇨ Inability to love without hesitation.
- ⇨ Failure to listen sincerely to one another.
- ⇨ Lack of *mutual respect* and *moral responsibility.*
- ⇨ Failure to make the relationship (love) the priority.

❤ Making Love a Priority

The last reason, failure to make our relationship (love) a priority, often creates confusion because we are unsure how this request fits into our busy and often overwhelming lives. Moreover, we are uncertain to what extent our relationships have to become a priority. Do we have to drop everything at any given time and become absorbed in our relationship at all times? If our first thought in the morning and our last thought at night does not revolve around our partner, are we guilty of neglect? Most importantly, we are not sure how to balance our remaining priorities, if this relationship is to be our first priority.

Just as love does not happen by accident, making our relationship a priority is a conscious choice and an act of our free will. There is a big difference between seeing our partners as relentlessly demanding people in our lives, and happily prioritizing quality time to spend with them to create intimacy and security in our relationships. Once we consciously decide to make our love a priority, our actions clearly become those that foster and nourish relationships. In the process we create trust, depth and commitment for our partners and ourselves. Our relationships become a source of energy.

Often when we observe couples in strong, loving relationships, we tend to think they simply hit it off or are very compatible. In truth, those relationships do not happen by accident. Instead, they are the result of a conscious choice to make love a priority.

Just as love should be a priority, so should the realization of your authentic self as discussed earlier. Once unveiled, it is that part in you which seeks a liberated life of love, dignity and accord. Unfortunately, most of what we do or say in a relationship is at odds with our authentic self, since most of our conduct is calculated to seek admiration and recognition. While this is understandable in a world that seems to reward only those with sought-after traits, time after time we enter into a relationship in a disguise and with false expectations. Then we are surprised that it didn't work out, again! In the end, we become powerless to resolve relationship difficulties, regardless of the potential for saving the relationship.

❤ 5 Principles to Remember from Chapter Five

1. The authentic self is the absolute manifestation of you.
2. You can blossom where you have been planted.
3. It is easy to love that which you do not know.
4. Multiple relationships are nothing but passing chapters in one's life.
5. Your true self does not disrespect, exploit or deceive others.

CHAPTER 6

LOVE McDONALD'S STYLE
Fast, Cheap and Easy

> *What we really need is a McShake-Up.*
> —Author Unknown

IN THE PREVIOUS CHAPTER, the discussion of authenticity was targeted at removing all the layers of pretense, play-acting and personality adjustments to allow the true self to emerge. We must all nurture the authentic self and expand our loving spirits of integrity and honesty. Growth of this kind is badly needed in a society where alienation, isolation, disaffection and division produce more sick people than most other recognized diseases. How long will it take until we realize love is the universal remedy for everyone?

> *Love received and love given comprise the best form of therapy.*
> —Gordon William Allport (1897–1967)
>   American Psychologist

Without love in our lives, everything else has much less meaning. Every time we foster our real self with its boundless power to love everyone, we release loving energy into the universe by touching those around us with our most precious gift: Our genuine loving self.

In our society we are, regrettably, more concerned with the *McDonaldization* of love. The simple rationale enslaving most of us has been that everything we do must ensure assessable rewards such as money, appreciation or a variety of other paybacks. Communally we relate similar principles in the area of love. We are not ready to love unless there is love in return. Loving for the sake of loving is a foreign concept for most of us. We have learned to attach our willingness to love to its projected rewards. It requires revolutionary thinking to open up to love and assert it in our lives. This mission is demanding, but always worth the effort, because without love our hearts will never be at peace. We love so much less than we are capable of loving. In fact, our hearts remain underutilized at the same time as humankind starves for love.

Increasingly, people everywhere wander from one relationship to another searching for love. Still, many singles have not had a date within the past year. Among those who did, many have slept with people with whom they normally wouldn't even have lunch with. Many in relationships are just a stone's throw away from becoming single again because of unresolved conflicts and built-up resentment.

> *Love is open arms. If you close your arms about love, you will find that you are left holding only yourself.*
> —Author Unknown

❤ McChicks and McStuds at the All-You-Can-Eat Buffet

At the *McLove-Drive-Thru,* singles everywhere are lining up and are doing everything in their power to become a desirable object, worthy of love and admiration. This enforces the widespread belief that love will come easily to those who can be identified on the menu as the right love object. Another pervasive belief is that success in finding love depends on the menu selection at the drive-thru. Even though the objective is to find love, emphasis seems to be placed on pursuing an object that meets socially defined and accepted criteria. Priority is given to the benefits and rewards received from the object of love, rather than on one's own capacity to love.

Singles enter this commodity market expecting to find a person who closely resembles their criteria of what is desirable, while at the same time trying to place themselves on the menu. This brings us to the subject of how to get posted on the menu, or in short, how to become the most wanted *McChick* or *McStud*.

In helping singles find partners, attractiveness has been the predominantly sought after characteristic. Attractiveness in this sense refers to how the person is packaged and presented. Attractiveness of women implies being beautiful, slender, youthful, feminine, confident, intelligent and independent and preferably financially secure. Much of the same holds true for men, who are expected to be tall, handsome, fit, smart, to some extent powerful, with an emphasis on being financially independent. Additionally, men and women both seek honesty, communication, trust, care and some level of commitment. Surprisingly, these human qualities are ignored at the drive-thru and the absence of them is not realized until well into a relationship.

Because of slick marketing in a society that constantly defines the image of an attractive mate, many singles ignore the human attributes required in a loving relationship. As much as we want to deny it, whom we choose on the menu has never been a matter of free choice. With the exception of a few, we are influenced, if not controlled by, the social standards of youth, thinness and eternal beauty. The media saturates us daily with today's beauty ideals to the point of taking over our minds and regulating our selection process. The inescapable influence of media icons blessed with perfect bodies and eternal youth has manufactured the belief that the most rewards go to the young, beautiful, handsome, fit and financially independent.

Today's young, slim and trim beauty images suggest that our bodies and faces are deficient and that we ought to restore, preserve, undo and reclaim that which comes effortlessly to media models. Singles spend millions of dollars, valuable time and tremendous effort trying to reach the threshold of visual acceptance. In an attempt to fit this mold and by disciplining their bodies, many have gone beyond exercising and eating right only to fall victims to the tyranny of thinness and trimness. Women outnumber men in the weight-loss war, and even the slim constantly fear weight-gain. Demoralizing facial lines must be attacked by an unlimited number of facial products designed to make older skin behave and look younger. Gray hair must be hidden under dyes, lost hair must be replaced with new follicles and unwanted body hair must be removed from inappropriate places. Clothing must conform to the latest fashion prescriptions, and women need to display cleavage to its greatest advantage. While some image improvement is often needed to feel better, much more is done to compete in the love commodity market.

Today's women wear false eyelashes, fake fingernails, layers of balancing, perfecting, illuminating and concealing make-up, bras which have lives of their own and subject themselves to a variety of "corrective" surgeries. The irony is that much of this "repackaging" is done in search of *McStud*. It is not surprising, then, that in the pursuit of obtaining this socially constructed synthetic image many are destined to fail and their bodies become their enemies.

This conformity imbedded in the *McValue* concept fosters a silent policing. We compare ourselves to others and, at the same time, we judge them. Those who do not measure up are struck from the menu and labeled unfit, undesirable or past their "best before" date.

Attractive people are seen as friendlier, more interesting, more sexually responsive and more likeable. Because they enjoy greater social endorsement they are given more attention and greater opportunities than less attractive people. Our mates, companions and those with whom we keep company are a reflection of who we are. Consequently, a relationship with an attractive partner promises many social rewards, such as elevating one's own desirability, increasing self-esteem and gaining respect.

Considerable research on the subject of attributing mainly positive qualities to attractive people has been done in the field of social psychology. People who hold traditional beliefs about genders often engage in attractiveness stereotyping, the belief that "what is beautiful is also good." In contrast, those who hold more egalitarian views of relationships are more likely to not judge a book by its cover.

From an evolutionary perspective, men and women seek healthy mates in order to produce healthy offspring. We tend to believe that physically attractive people are more likely to be healthy than unattractive people. A study of mating strategies suggests that physical attractiveness and possession of resources were judged important in selecting a long-term mate, whereas sexual availability and generosity seemed to be more important in short term affairs. These findings would explain why singles worldwide advertise their level of physical attractiveness combined with financial stability or independence. It appears that beauty, wealth and power continue to be highly valued attributes, and more people are seeking these attributes than there are those who are able to provide them. Consequently, those who have beauty, power and wealth determine the price at which they are trading.

Rational Choice Theory extends the law of "diminishing utility" into human psychology. This law states that as the consuming of desirable goods increases, its marginal utility (the extra utility that one gains by consuming another unit of the good) tends to decrease and so does the amount we are willing to pay for it. For example, when you are very thirsty you are prepared to pay almost anything for your first cold drink. The second drink will be worth much less to you and you might decline it if it is too expensive. Applying this principle of diminishing utility to the *McLove-Drive-Thru*, we become aware that if all "love candidates" possessed beauty, power and wealth, our obsession with these qualities would diminish. In light of the abundance of these traits, we would actually pay attention to the character traits, beliefs and values of people before we made our selection.

The commonly cited phenomenon of the "Trophy Wife" refers to the tendency of successful and wealthy men to typically choose women younger than themselves on the basis of beauty alone. Studies of singles ads over the past 25 years indicate this exchange of beauty for wealth. Women who can offer youth and attractiveness commonly seek men that offer financial security. These women have no problem with the men being older.

When I was younger I entertained the idea of finding a rich man, and I wanted to look like Barbie® to make my task less challenging. Instead, I had many of the same issues that trouble other young women. I was overweight with far from flawless skin. I could not figure out how to display my modest breasts, lacked a flattering wardrobe and my rebellious personality always collided with protocol. I concluded that I wasn't even close to Barbie® and, in retrospect, this might have been a blessing, since today the Barbie image is associated with an airhead, dumb enough to fail a blood test. Nevertheless, many women today, particularly those who are economically underprivileged, secretly wish to find love pooled with some form of economic improvement and just as many men, wealthy or not, still dream about their own version of Barbie®.

❤ Shall Birds of a Feather Flock Together?

It can also be difficult to find love because we seek someone who is similar to us in attitude and level of attractiveness. We may do this consciously or unconsciously, depending on which idea we buy into: that "birds of a feather flock together" or "opposites attract."

Our mood also influences how attractive we feel. The more positive we feel about life, the higher we rate our attractiveness, and the more attractiveness we radiate to others. We benefit in more ways than one when we maintain a positive outlook and keep smiling as we greet the world each day.

Most people rate themselves as better looking than others would and as a result seek partners who are either as attractive as they think they are or more so. Very few are interested in dating someone who they consider to be less attractive than they are. Attractiveness also refers to a person's fashion sense, grooming habits and how self-assured he or she is. Most people prefer to date someone with a level of sophistication close to their own. When we overrate ourselves, we are often quick to downgrade another person, which in turn can lead to very unrealistic expectations.

Single or not, many are unfortunately stuck on the idea that love is to be found in the right package, and that more attractive people are more deserving of being loved. Moreover, we seem to be persuaded by the idea that a relationship ought to benefit us, and we evaluate people on the basis of their advantage to us. With our "What's in it for me?" attitude about relationships we are often surprised when yet another relationship fails.

> *Ask not what your partner can do for you, ask what you can do for your partner.*
> —Author: Not John F. Kennedy

In truth, we all need to be loved, not for who others expect us to be but for who we are and will become, because of love. We need to look at the special person we are instead of how we compare to others. We also need to look at other human beings just as non-judgmentally as we would like to be regarded.

I have discussed at length the importance we place on attractiveness when selecting a partner and pointed out how misguided our perceptions in this area are. Nearly everyone at the drive-thru is yearning for the most perfect and the least flawed person. With such a short supply of perfect people (if any), it becomes evident that most walk away from the drive-thru feeling hungry. In truth, there are very few strikingly gorgeous people on this planet, just as there are very few truly ugly people. Most of us are average people with ordinary faults. Many of our so-called faults are not even true faults, but are merely characteristics we simply dislike in ourselves and others. Paradoxically, these imperfections make each one of us unique and special, and allow us to grow and learn from each other.

Are we attracted to people who are similar to us or to those who are quite different? These two opposing belief systems can give many singles a one-directional view when seeking a partner. Most research indicates that the majority are drawn to those with similar attitudes, beliefs, preferences and world-views. Keep in mind that research and its general statements apply to the population at large and deviations are always possible.

We are attracted to people with similar attitudes for a number of reasons:

- ⇨ It requires less effort to get to know the person.
- ⇨ Our minds are less challenged by a person with similar attitudes, and we experience a relaxed interaction.
- ⇨ Our own attitudes are validated when someone else shares them.
- ⇨ Similar attitudes produce liking, and reduce anxieties associated with rejection.
- ⇨ When someone holds similar attitudes and beliefs we can often predict the person's behavior.

If you know that someone has a significant interest in computers you can often predict that the person is interested in technology, perceives technology as beneficial, uses the Internet, spends much time on the computer and that a computer trade show would be his or her idea of an enjoyable outing. On the negative side, some may go as far as to assume this person is a nerd, anti-social, has poor communication skills and is emotionally withdrawn. Knowing the attitude or preference of someone tempts us to make various inferences about the person, be they negative or positive. Even if we have minimal information, we often make quick judgments and form impressions about others through stereotyping. When we meet people for the first time we classify them as belonging to particular groups, such as male, female, black, white, computer nerds, outdoor lovers, white collar, blue collar, sports fanatics, educated or not. We then act upon the belief that the person has certain characteristics common to all members of whatever groups we associate them with. For example, all men are competitive, dominant and un-emotional; all women are sensitive, dependent and less competitive. Computer nerds are socially challenged, blue-collar workers are less sophisticated than white collar, and Italians are great lovers and gigolos. Our acquired biases form our first impressions of those we meet and greatly influence our decision whether to give these people any further attention. Even though stereotyping is helpful when mentally organizing our social encounters, often our biases produce inaccurate impressions. These inaccurate perceptions can either mislead us into inappropriate liaisons, or preclude experience with an exceptional human being.

❤ Dumb Founded

As identical twins, Melissa and Melanie were brought up in a nurturing and stable upper class family with both parents maintaining professional careers. Now, at the age of 26, Melissa is a nurse and Melanie an urban developer. Both are looking for Mr. Right and their ideals are as identical as they are: tall, handsome, fit, educated, of similar socio-economic background, successful, caring, committed, socially desirable and much more. Both believe that the more similar their partner would be, the greater their chance of relationship success.

When Melissa visited a bar with her girlfriends, young Daryl took to her. He sent a drink to her table and later introduced himself. Melissa and her girlfriends had already decided that even though Daryl was good-looking, the fact that he hung out at the bar wearing a baseball cap, drinking beer and watching football was clear evidence that he was not in their league. When it became known that Daryl was a factory worker, Melissa decided that he would never be on her "must-date" list. During her brief encounter with Daryl, Melissa focused only on information that confirmed her stereotyping of factory workers and ignored information to the contrary. To her, all factory workers were uneducated slobs, wore baseball caps, were only interested in sports, lacked social skills and were too embarrassing to introduce to friends and family. Melissa thought herself to be of higher quality and dismissed Daryl as unworthy of her consideration. Like so many of us with prejudice she paid a hefty price for her erroneous generalization.

Months later, her sister Melanie announced she had met a wonderful man whom she would like to introduce to her family. This man was Daryl, who, to Melissa's surprise, turned out to be capable of intelligent and interesting conversation on topics other than sports, survived the evening without a baseball cap and his trustworthy, lively personality won major points with her parents. Over the course of the following year, Melissa saw her sister happier than ever. This wonderful, kind, funny and sincere man brought love and happiness to her sister's life and joy and laughter to the entire family. The family was thrilled when they married. Daryl would never be the highly sophisticated individual of equal social status that Melissa aspired to meet. He still enjoys watching sports and sharing a few beers with his friends while proudly wearing his baseball cap. Daryl is a sensitive, respectful and attentive husband who has so much love to give his wife and their child. He is an awesome brother-in-law to Melissa, who recognizes the great fortune her sister found in sharing her life with Daryl. There is a lesson to be learned from Melissa's story: Opportunities are never lost; someone else will take those that you miss.

Jake was attracted to Gail because she held many of the same attitudes and beliefs as he did and was at his level of attractiveness. Gail enjoyed working out, bicycling, playing tennis, golfing and skiing, and had an otherwise active and healthy lifestyle. For

Jake, sharing these kinds of things was extremely important. By the time Gail and Jake married, their lives revolved around working out, staying in shape, eating right and keeping each other in check. Being dedicated to health and fitness is definitely admirable; however, their dedication became an addiction and the main focus of their relationship. Their limited perception of each other coupled with an inadequate vision of their shared life left them short of a truly meaningful relationship. Jake was not prepared for the day when their pervasive similarities and a shared lifestyle addiction would come to an end.

After five years of marriage Jake severely injured his back. His fitness schedule became limited and eventually it was impossible for him to participate in the activities he previously shared with Gail. As his back pain worsened, he was unable to continue working. Consequently, their finances shrank and he began to suffer from depression. The deterioration of his physical and emotional state, combined with their altered finances presented a disagreeable burden for Gail and stalled her lifestyle. She saw Jake as a sick, weak, weight-gaining person, who fell short of her ideal. He no longer fit her bill. Gail filed for divorce, leaving Jake to wonder whether he had heard, "in sickness and in health" or "in slenderness and in wealth."

Some of you may condemn Gail while others may sympathize with her. I could devote an entire book to an analysis of the alleged vagueness of this specific marriage vow. Maybe this vow should define for us how sick we can get or how healthy we have to be, to make it stick in its conditional version. It appears that over 60 percent of the population has come to appreciate conditional marriage vows over the unconditional.

Think back to the six points set out earlier in this chapter that explained why we seek those of similar attitudes, beliefs, values and lifestyles. All those reasons apply to Jake and Gail, and as a result their relationship had been comfortable, non-confrontational, validating, effortless, relaxed and highly predictable. Sounds like smooth sailing so far. Prior to Jake's injury they experienced very little conflict and felt validated because they shared common priorities. In reality they did not know the important things about one another. They only challenged each other on their fitness levels and nutritional regimes, not on becoming better human beings. They lived superficially within their comfort zones and the absence of conflict prevented the growth of their relationship. I am not suggesting that one should provoke conflict; however, relationships that are able to resolve conflict will grow stronger. It is only by getting to know the person behind the mask and extending beyond the superficiality of the relationship that we learn to respect each other. Gail and Jake managed to sustain an uneventful and somewhat gratifying relationship, but underneath, the foundation was unstable. Like a house of cards, each time we build on a shaky foundation our relationship is destined to tumble.

I was a conflict avoider myself and sought friends and mates among those who were similar to me. I encountered minimal conflict and my mind was left unchallenged. My like-minded friends validated my beliefs, views and attitudes about the world and the people in it. As a matter of fact, I had it all figured out and there was little anyone could tell me. I was in my comfort zone with only one problem: I did not learn much about the world outside of my personal frame of reference. I was closed-minded, judgmental, had strong convictions and, in essence, I did not grow as a person.

At the age of 25, I left my comfort zone in Germany together with my beliefs about life. I immigrated lock, stock and barrel to Canada where my beliefs about life, the world and people were challenged. In my old life, I had avoided people who were different from me, but living in this new country I no longer could. Every day I came across people living different lifestyles, holding different beliefs, values and attitudes. I realized that I was given an intellect to use it to its fullest potential, and that I could only learn, absorb, respect, appreciate and identify with others if my mind was open. As I gained a wealth of newfound knowledge, I understood that everything that I was, am and will be is because of my relationships with others. I became implicitly aware that most of my significant personal development was due to opening my heart to those who were different from me.

When we approach relationships with an emphasis on finding a similar person, we are most likely to find comfort and validation. When we broaden our vision to include different people, we will definitely find challenges, maybe even confrontations and most certainly conflicts. It is through challenges and conflicts that we grow, flourish, mature and become better human beings.

❤ Attitude Adjustment

Our attitudes include feelings and evaluations about whether something is good or bad, and consequently they guide our behavior. They are important to us because they represent who we think we are, deliver cues to others about us and define how we perceive the world. We need to form attitudes and beliefs about people and situations to evaluate our environment and those around us. We learn from our parents and peers what to believe in and what attitudes to hold. We are rewarded when we adopt their beliefs, and we are disciplined if we maintain contradictory views. However, many of our beliefs and attitudes are merely generalized statements or stereotypes, often lacking sufficient proof or information. Many of the beliefs and attitudes we hold lead to assumptions about others that couldn't be further from the truth and, sadly, keep us from finding the relationships we seek.

What will it take to stir your soul? What will it take to recognize that you are not meant to chase after love, but to identify all the barricades and defenses within yourself that get in the way of love? Regardless of how narrow-minded your beliefs about others may be, people can be enthused, encouraged, inspired, motivated, reclaimed, transformed, recharged, replenished, rejuvenated and beautified in the face of love.

Hundreds of singles were asked, "Would you want your partner to be like you?" The answer was "No." These same singles were asked to describe their ideal partner and the results were stunning: The majority described someone very similar to themselves. These findings support the previous claim that we believe it's easier to have relationships with those who are very similar to us and relationships with those who are dissimilar produce conflict. The fact that we are indeed looking for someone very much like ourselves is evident in the numerous proclamations from singles: "I am looking for my soul-mate." Time after time the term "soul-mate" is misinterpreted as someone with whom we can have the perfect, conflict-free, effortless relationship in which we understand each other intuitively.

The longer singles remain single and hold the belief that similarities are a guarantee for lasting relationships; the less likely they are to find love. Because of this mindset, singles often miss out on wonderful relationships with people who are quite different. Similarly, in troubled relationships and marriages, the longer partners believe that their problems are due to their differences, the more likely they are to leave and join the circle of singles just described. Love does not require similarity of views and attitudes, nor does it require perfection. Instead it accepts differences, opposing views, imperfections, baggage and conflict.

All of us see this world not as it is, but from our own limited perspective. That is exactly why we do not share a universal reality. Learning to live with the differences of our present partners, and those we are about to meet, gives us richer resources, greater wisdom, diverse knowledge and a clearer perception of reality.

❤ Love at First Bite

I would now like to focus on our misguided ideas of what love is and where it can be found. You have probably heard more advice about how and where to meet someone than I would ever want to give. When you finally did meet someone "special" you heard even more advice on how to keep love and romance alive. The advice over the years has changed, in that it has become more philosophical and expanded to include new, technologically driven methods through which we meet. For couples the advice has changed in light of altered economic circumstances, new research and the quest for almost perfect relationships. We live in a society that seems to require "new and improved" everything, and has a constant need to make even great things better. It is no surprise that relationships should follow the same path.

Love is the number one topic of discussion, and the number one reason people seek advice is relationships. Almost all songs, regardless of category, are about love. The entire entertainment industry revolves around love and we are paying big bucks to watch others making love for us at the same time as they are defining our love standards and ideals.

While the love sold by the entertainment industry is only for the moment, it does not prevent us from investing our emotions and perceptions heavily in industry-defined love. Our love images are socially generated, and this idealistic view of romantic love is unique to our culture. We have learned that with love we are to experience arousal, desire, chemistry, joy, sexual attraction and euphoria and nothing less than that. We have come to acknowledge ideal notions of love, which often misguide our conduct.

1. Love at First Sight

Wouldn't it be marvelous if all you ever have to do is to be at the right place, at the right time to meet the right person and love would strike like a lightning bolt? Your prayers would be answered and love would never again be a mystery. The two of you would live happily ever after. Most of us are sensible enough to recognize that love does not happen this way, despite what we see in movies, on TV or read in novels. On movie screens we watch as love at first sight brightens those glamorous faces — heavily made up and for the most part the product of countless surgical adjustments. Ordinary people confess that their relationships began because of love at first sight, and some believe this to be the reason for their gratifying relationships.

Upon further inquiry, I established that all of these people either believed in love at first sight, or believed that they were destined to be with their partner by the grace of God. Others simply made their love a priority in their lives. These various perceptions of love account for their efforts to make their respective relationships work. Let's face it: If you believe in "love at first sight" and presume yourself struck by it, this belief by both partners creates a joint perception that the relationship is to be treasured. Consequently, together they cherish, respect and nurture this union to their utmost ability. By the same token, when two people meet believing themselves to be *fit to love*, it stands to reason that they have both investigated love closely and have less superficial notions about love than most do. By definition, those who are ready are also willing to accept the journey of love, for better or worse and nothing less.

For those who believe in God's delivery of love, their relationships are sacred right from the start, and are guided by faith, trust and destiny. When faced with the trials and tribulations they are not alone in holding together that which God has joined. The belief in God is relevant to their intentions, and often those who do believe in God (or a spiritual being) have a greater chance of becoming *fit to love*.

Does "love at first sight" exist? I am not convinced that it does. I go so far as to claim it is impossible. I believe that any emotion associated with love does exist at first sight, be it arousal, attraction, fascination, desire, lust or the need to be loved. These emotions can become overpowering in the presence of someone who evokes these feelings in us. People who claim to have loved at first sight have far deeper underlying beliefs and perceptions of love and relationships. What all of them have in common is the willingness to love another person and to set in motion what most of us perceive to be the risks involved in loving. They believe that once they have chosen the person, through whatever belief system, fate will be on their side while their relationships develop into abundant experiences of love. Love at first sight may not exist, but the willingness to experience it does.

As wonderful as it may be to believe in love at first sight, this belief can also be counterproductive. Love is not a stationary product that can be attained by looking into someone's eyes, nor is it the property of an individual. The fact that both of you stared into each other's eyes at the same time as your favorite song played has nothing to do with love. The idea of love at first sight turns easily into *love on the first night*. The phrase "Look before you leap" should mean, "Look before you strip" your clothes and soul, for love is so much more patient than your hormones will ever be.

2. There is only one right person for everyone in this world.

This belief is very convenient for procrastinators who are afraid of making a decision to love, and instead are simply waiting for the right person. There is no better time to procrastinate than right now. Singles who buy into this notion see the wrong person in everyone, and the search for the right person seems more stimulating than the actual find. Convinced that they have more to offer than the rest of the world, they believe they are among the best catches within a 500 mile radius and behave accordingly.

They are members of the growing cult of the self-absorbed, who see themselves as the winning tickets of the century; they devaluate others, and believe better alternatives are always available. With the number of singles steadily growing in our globe of abundance, these people obviously feel justified investing in their egos but not in their hearts.

More than anything else the belief that there is only one right person for each of us is a reflection of a person's unrealistic expectations. The fear of committing to the wrong person is greater than their trust in their intuitions. They demand more than they can give and even though they claim to know what they are after, they never seem to find it.

In truth, there are many right people for you. In fact, the idea that there is only one right person is an illusion, especially if you consider your "right person" will change over time anyway. Most of us would like to find the right person and when we do, we hope this person never changes. But people do change and not always the way we like. Everyone changes physically, emotionally and mentally and if you find it difficult to accept change, I suggest you ship yourself to a taxidermist.

3. I know within 10 minutes of meeting someone if they are worth pursuing.

"Crash-dating" suggests we have the ability to assess another human being within ten minutes. Since not even a well-trained psychiatrist or employer is capable of making this assessment, what makes some of us think we can? When on a date we may put more importance into wardrobe selection than we do for a job interview, but we certainly bring less information to a date than we do to an interview.

The idea that we can size up a person within minutes is ludicrous, because all we can observe is appearance, some behavior, eye contact, manner and speech. Add to that the fact that most people tell enormous lies on first encounters to create enough interest for a second date, and you really don't know a whole lot. On these "Power Dates" we are victims of our expectations, and the feedback we receive confirms what we believe or disbelieve about the person. Our date is under as much stress as we are and seeks to create an outstanding first impression. Our subjective judgments prevent us from observing the other person in an objective manner. In this anxiety-producing situation nobody shows their true colors, and the impressions we form of one another are inaccurate and obscure.

The common declaration "If I am not attracted to the person, what is the point?" is responsible for many snap decisions based on one thing only: attraction. We may be attracted to the person's body shape, eyes, smile, hair, voice and gestures, which may produce the chemistry, which we believe to be so important. However, chemistry, like many other experiences, is a matter of borrowed time. The chemistry we feel for a person to whom we are superficially attracted fades very quickly, particularly when we discover nothing else desirable about them. We fail to realize that we are attracted to the feeling this person creates in us, not the actual person. For example, Malcolm prides himself on having dated the most gorgeous women, but he never found love. He did not gain anything other than an inflated ego, and has no meaningful memories to look back on. Fortunately he changed his counterproductive conduct, and now handles the souls of others as well as his own with more care.

I have seen many people fall in love with each other even though there was no initial chemistry. I have seen just as many people, who after a friendship without romance, fell in love with the core of the other person and subsequently developed chemistry. The idea that there must be chemistry at the onset is often misleading. Just as initial chemistry can fade when we discover disagreeable traits in the other person (most of us have been there), chemistry can emerge when we honor and respect the core of another. "Crash dating" as described above is, more often than not, very much like crash dieting, which is unsustainable and leaves us starving.

4. Love conquers all.

Most likely it will not. Love means different things to different people. Only *mutual respect* for and *moral responsibility* to one another have a universal meaning. In the absence of respect and responsibility, love is merely an arbitrary term. The romantic idea that all difficulties can be sealed with a kiss brings to mind a love song. Not surprisingly, this song is still one of the most popular and powerful wedding songs. When Brian Adams sings at the top of his lungs, "Everything I Do (I Do It for You)," thousands of people look at each other and many hope to experience love to some degree as depicted in the song. Truthfully, most of us have been socialized to be self-interested and to expect rewards for what we do, even when we love. Everything we do, we do mostly for ourselves. The lyrics should read "Everything I do, I do it for me or wait until you do it."

"*I'd fight for you.*" It sounds very heroic, but let there be no mistake, most of us are too chicken to fight for our own beliefs and causes, let alone for someone else's. While many people, single or not, are bleeding from invisible wounds they are very reluctant to stand up for another person. Apart from stage fright, we are very much confused about what to believe in and what to fight for.

"*I'd lie for you.*" Apart from the fact that lying has become very acceptable in relationships, not to mention among presidents and prime ministers, you might have much better luck finding someone who lies to you instead of for you.

"*I'd die for you.*" As passionate as it may appear, you have a much better chance of being killed in a relationship if you are heavily life-insured, than of finding someone who will put his or her life on the line for you. Humanists, like Mahatma Gandhi and Nelson Mandela, who risked their lives in the name of freedom and justice, are few and far between. Even though their love did not conquer all, surely they showed us that we need a different kind of love if we are to conquer anything at all.

Where there is love there is life.
—MAHATMA GANDHI

Brian Adams's song demonstrates our mainly romantic notion of love. That romantic notion is confirmed by the huge sales of Harlequin romance novels as well as Danielle Steele's more upscale version of the same thing.

As much as my assessment of how we interpret love is an exaggeration, the way we understand love today is by no means enough to conquer all. We need a different love or we will lose the battle not only in our individual relationships but also collectively. Through this book you will be introduced to this different kind of love that entails all of humanity. You will see that anything worthwhile in this world happens through this love, including meaningful relationships.

If you find yourself either at the *McLove-Drive-Thru*, almost single, half-heartedly involved, married or in the midst of divorce (a pending candidate for the *McLove-Drive-Thru*), consider what you have read so far. Hopefully you will understand that for the most part we expect far more of others than we are willing to give. In other words, what we want most in our relationships is also what we are the least willing to give. We need to love others and ourselves guided by *mutual respect* and *moral responsibility*, because only then can we be sure that this love will not disappear.

Love is the only thing that lets us see each other with the remotest accuracy.
—MARTHA BECK

❤ 5 Principles to Remember from Chapter Six

1. There is power and growth in conflict.
2. Your attitudes and beliefs guide your behavior.
3. Not everything you believe about the world and people is true.
4. Crash dates are like crash diets—they leave you hungry.
5. Love entails all of humanity.

CHAPTER 7

I LOVE ME; WHOM DO YOU LOVE?
If I Love You, Will I Get the Goody Bag?

> *Love is not something that you have;*
> *it is something that you do.*
> —Author Unknown

WITH OVER A BILLION SERVED, we certainly have *McDonaldized* our concept of ideal love, so why shouldn't we have our "treat of the week?" Singles are particularly receptive to *McDonaldization* simply because they see themselves as struggling to survive in a competitive market. Youth in women, wealth in men, slenderness, attractiveness, sexiness and fashion are marketed and promoted not merely as socially desirable attributes but as happiness-producing qualities. Even when these standards change, they change along with them. Someone becomes worthy of pursuit based on these standards that are both the primary enticements for entering a relationship and the gauge for its anticipated success. These standards drive the expectations they have of others and themselves and consequently they become experts in managing their social identities. In fact, social competitiveness causes most of us to engage in *calculated impression management*. This is evident by the clothes we wear, the restaurants we like, the books we read, the homes we live in, the cars we drive, the activities we choose, and the opinions we defend, all of which support the identities we portray to others. We play deceptive roles in order to be liked and respected by those whose approval we seek.

❤ If Life Is a Game, Let's Change the Rules

Fear of rejection is a strong incentive for *calculated impression management,* and is very common among dating singles. On a first date, it is important that the other person likes them and is attracted to them even if it turns out that they have no interest in the other. Conversely, when they are interested in someone who does not return this interest, they conclude that there is something wrong with the judgment of the other person. The thought that it is possible for a perfectly normal person not to like them is unacceptable, as this possibility attacks their fragile ego. As they become obsessed with what others think of them, they manage their portrayed identities by exaggerating their good points while obscuring their flaws.

The well-known sociologist, Erving Goffman (1922–1982), looked in depth at the identities and the behaviors that people present to others. He viewed life as a staged drama with human actors playing out roles and following scripts based on social structures. In using a theater analogy, *Front* and *Back Stage* behavior, he explains how we act out our roles. *Front Stage* behavior refers to the behavior we display for others in an effort to achieve a positive evaluation. On the *Front Stage* we are performing actors who manipulate our viewers and listeners. At the *Back Stage,* hidden from our audience, we practice our *Front Stage* behavior but are people without social masks. Even though our *Back Stage* behavior is accessible to those close to us, we know how to fool even them and will do so for two reasons:

1. We are afraid they will no longer love us if they become aware of all our *Back Stage* behavior.

2. We fear that the rewards we receive, be they material or emotional, will change or discontinue if our entire self becomes exposed.

The second reason explains why people feel more comfortable showing their real self when a relationship is about to break up and another candidate is in the wings to deliver rewards. The discrepancies between *Front Stage* impression management and *Back Stage* behavior can be extreme and have far-reaching consequences.

Phil Drillfill, a methodical spick-and-span dentist, thrived on sophisticated cooking feats and extended grocery-shopping sprees. In fact, he commonly devoted much more time to preparing one meal than most of us would spend preparing meals for an entire week. When a young, beautiful and slim Jennifer replied to his personal ad (drawn to his professional status), Dr. Drillfill thought the Tooth Fairy had touched-down. She claimed to share his passion for gourmet cooking and home life, but, because of her young children, opted to delay inviting him to her home. During their courtship they enjoyed dining in fine restaurants or at Phil's home. As Jennifer successfully presented the image of a great cook and meticulous housekeeper, Phil liked her even more. The inevitable moment of discovery arrived when Phil landed on her doorstep to surprise her with flowers. The visit to Jennifer's home was a startling revelation for which Phil was not prepared. An equally startled and rather embarrassed Jennifer reluctantly opened the door to her home that fairly resembled a pigsty. Apart from the trail of children's debris that littered her kitchen, fridge magnets and fridge notes read: "A clean, well stocked kitchen is a sign of a wasted life," "Martha Stewart doesn't live here" and "I will vacuum when they come out with a riding model."

Phil felt disappointed and betrayed. He had grown very fond of her and could have compromised in the areas of housekeeping and cooking. However, he was unable to get over her misrepresentation, and was suspicious that she might have deceived him in other areas of her personality as well. Needless to say, their promising relationship ended. Jennifer accused Phil of being a "neat-freak" in order to rationalize her deception. Even though they had been off to a good start, their affection for one another turned into resentment.

Is it possible for a relationship such as Phil and Jennifer's to succeed? Certainly it is, but only if they acknowledge that they misrepresent themselves out of fear that they are not lovable enough. Jennifer misled Phil because she felt she had to measure up on certain fronts to be accepted. Phil misled Jennifer by telling her he had not dated for some time until she came along. He had expected Jennifer to remain exclusively available to him even though he continued to see other women. He was disrespectful of Jennifer, although she never learned of his deception.

Many of the rules defining what is acceptable while dating or while in full-fledged relationships are made without regard to *mutual respect* or the fact that we are indeed morally responsible to those whose emotions and lives we affect. With their strong affections and much in common (forget the cooking and cleaning) Phil and Jennifer could have allowed their conflict to become the seed for growth. Instead, single again and disappointed, Phil continues to miss Jennifer while pursuing his almost sanitary life. Jennifer misses Phil as well, but their pride and inability to compromise ended their relationship.

When we truly respect another we are able to see the other

person's perspective, which then allows us to compromise on honorable terms rather than for selfish reasons. The story of Jennifer and Phil is an example of how relationships that begin with deception end after a short time. The cleanliness conflict could have been any other issue that could have been solved through compromise. However, far too many people believe, "If there are any compromises to be made, you had better make them!"

Our reluctance to compromise is rooted in beliefs we hold throughout our lives. How dare another person challenge our beliefs or, even worse, ask us to compromise? While the human spirit can never compromise on moral principles and integrity, many of the conflicts responsible for the epidemic *relationship-hopping* could be resolved by compromise. In the case of Jennifer and Phil, the compromise would have been rather straightforward even though both ranked cleanliness on a different scale. Love does not care whether a house is clean, only people do, and this holds true for many trivial issues in love and life. Jennifer need not wait for a riding vacuum cleaner and Phil could go easy on the cleaning products. As for the cooking issues, there is merit in both gourmet style and simple home fare, right down to hot dogs. Does this solution sound too simple for you? Well, it is simple because when there is love, there is *mutual respect* and when there is respect, there is compromise on human terms.

❤ I Love You if You Love Me First

Some people enter relationships thinking "Anything good that will happen, better happen to me first." This statement addresses the trend among love-seekers to hold back in a relationship until there is evidence beyond any reasonable doubt that their lover is hooked. Typically they withhold affection in relatively new relationships out of fear of receiving less love than they give. When both withhold love until all the evidence is in, they never conclude beyond a reasonable doubt that the other person loves them. They keep each other on probation. Aloofness and a guarded self may be considered protection for our fragile egos, allowing us to appear independent, but in reality, they hinder intimacy and growth.

Socially created images have taught us what love should be, how it should feel and how we should feel when we are in love. These images also inform us what our lovers are supposed to do and say when they are in love with us. We are well equipped to scrutinize one another for evidence of loving us as well as for signs to the contrary. We have accepted icons and symbols of love and our interpretations of hard evidence of love are quite diverse. Relationships often end because we conclude that we either love more than the other, or that there is no hope in Hell for reciprocal love, even when neither situation is true.

Why do we withhold love until we are sure of receiving enough love in return to make it worthwhile? The obvious motivator is fear. In fact, we have endless fears: of being hurt, taken advantage of, used, abused, exposed, humiliated, left alone, harassed, damaged, ruined, eroded, persuaded, tricked, depleted, sucked dry, stepped on, turned upside down, rolled over, run over, demolished, tarnished, deflated, discouraged, knocked over, pushed aside, tampered with, stalked, robbed, choked and eventually gunned down.

For the majority of us with weak egos, there is much at stake when we put our vulnerable hearts on the line. The present divorce rate translates into a failure of more than half of marriages, and this statistic doesn't even include the failed relationships of the unmarried. Even though it is a known fact that those in rewarding relationships are happier, healthier and more prosperous, those seeking meaningful relationships continue to be motivated by fear.

A meaningful relationship is based on a commitment to *mutual respect* and *moral responsibility*. These are big words and many do not understand their meaning or how they apply to a relationship. Instead, our culture endorses self-fulfillment at almost any cost. We are at the point where schools should soon grant degrees to those wishing to "major in themselves."

People everywhere are saddened by the difficulties in establishing meaningful relationships, but most seem unable to reach out. In particular, those with histories of failed relationships have acquired the self-defeating habit of approaching subsequent relationships as conditional undertakings. "I love you, if you love me first" means nothing less than "I am only willing to get burnt once I see you in flames," or " I am only setting my life off in a spin after you become dizzy." Placing conditions on relationships suggests that we want to control the power and maintain an advantage over the other person. It further indicates that the idea of a relationship of equality is still a foreign concept to many.

Regardless of the scientific or philosophical explanation to which we subscribe when explaining the differences among us, we must realize that we are humans first. This fact is the key to equality. Healthy relationships require equal power distribution, equal respect for each other's views, and equal responsibility to one another on a moral level.

Most of us are victims of conditional views of love, such as "If she loved me, she would lose 20 pounds," or "If he loved me, he would spend more time with me." This conditional approach is not only present in new relationships, but also in many long-term relationships, and it causes emotional insecurities. When we see and judge others through our expectations we keep track of how they measure up. We link the degree to which our partners meet our expectations to the amount of love or attraction we feel for them. In doing so, we fail to make a true assessment of the other person.

Often unaware, we operate on the principle of getting the most out of a relationship for the least input. If it looks like our input exceeds the output of the other, we wander off to the next relationship. Many times this cure is worse than the cause. It must be emphasized that you can love someone and not lose 20 pounds, or you can love someone and still enjoy spending time apart from that person.

No matter how much someone loves you, he or she will always do and say things from which you could infer not being loved enough. Simply because someone expresses love in a way other than what you expect, he or she may still love you wholeheartedly. While counseling relationships I have always been amazed by people's need to be the focus of their partner's attention. I concluded that because of our confused identities and frail egos, it makes us feel good to be the center of someone else's life. Often we believe that when our partners do more for us and less for themselves, they must love us more.

Love does not demand that we do everything for our partner, nor does it require us to give up our growth, development and interests. People do what they do for their own reasons, which may be different from our own, but their reasons are nevertheless just as valid. When we respect another person the way we respect ourselves, we will respect their reasons as much as our own. Unfortunately, even when we care about each other it does not follow that we respect each other. Often partners holding different opinions irritate us so much of the time that we make little effort to walk in their shoes. Instead, we tend to see our own views as superior. In our effort to be right, we defend our position and disrespect each other. Being right has become more important than finding middle ground.

Most of us are immersed in our own narrow thoughts that limit our understanding of others, prevent us from experiencing meaningful relationships and, in turn, become self-fulfilling prophecies of disappointment. Once you become aware of what and how you think, your need to be right and defensive no longer presents a barrier in your relationships. Through this book you will break new ground in the area of constructive thinking, a process that alleviates stress, anxiety, power struggles and insecurities in relationships. You can become free from needing people to be what you want them to be and love them for who they are. This is exactly how each of us wants to be loved.

❤ Conflict and Control

Conflict

Every time the concepts of *mutual respect* and *moral responsibility* are applied to relationship conflicts, resolution is achieved in the best interest of both parties. The following section deals with some common relationship issues and how these concepts may be applied to solve these issues.

1. Should you continue a relationship with an alcoholic who spends all your money and abuses you, just because you feel it necessary to respect his or her reasons and feel morally responsible?

Of course not! The fact that his or her behavior adversely impacts your life also deserves respect. Not only are you morally responsible to your partner, you are also responsible for yourself and to others you love. You can try to help your partner change his or her behavior in a loving, non-judgmental way, if he or she asks for your help. Many people recognize that they need to get better in order for their relationships to improve, and they do change in the face of unconditional love. If your partner does not see the need to take control over his or her addiction and its destructive consequences, you are then morally responsible for steering your partner in a curative direction, even if this means a separation until he or she is ready to take action.

Often people take a hard look at themselves in the face of a crisis or when confronting the prospect of losing someone they love. We all have a tremendous capacity to change, but for some it does take more than reason to achieve change. There is no point in faulting, judging, criticizing, or blaming the partner we would like to see change. This serves only to undermine remaining self-esteem, and steals faith in the ability to change. Everyone is capable of change although not everyone will. Change is more likely to occur if supported by love. Through encouragement and belief, we can give someone wings to fly beyond what they thought was possible. This is far more productive than criticism, even though the results are not guaranteed. While the issues of alcoholism or abuse are too complex to be fully addressed in this book, the concepts of respect, including self-respect and *moral responsibility*, should always lead us away from living miserable lives and, when necessary, guide us to professional help.

2. We love each other, but our conflicting interests create a lot of discord in our relationship.

This is the second summer in which Lucas spends most of his free time golfing. Karen dislikes golfing and would rather spend summer weekends at the beach with Lucas, a pastime that he finds terribly monotonous. On weekend evenings they either see a movie or go out for dinner, but their preferences are rather conflicting. Lucas enjoys science fiction and action movies, while Karen prefers comedy or love stories. He loves roadhouse food and she finds pleasure in fine cuisine. She is an early to bed and early to rise person, while Lucas enjoys late nights and dreads getting up early. Karen would love to live in a condo in the city with lots of shopping nearby and dislikes animals and yard work; Lucas dreams of living in the country with a large yard, dogs and cats.

Apart from opposing interests everything seems to be fine in their relationship. They enjoy each other, have fun, feel comfortable, trust each other and obviously really love each other. Is there hope? You bet! Respect for each other's likes and dislikes, dreams and hopes will tremendously enhance their respective views of life and expose them to a more enriching life experience. While Karen and Lucas differ in their preferences and opinions, there is no "right way" to live, eat, entertain or enjoy activities. Through willingness to see the positive in their diversities and embrace the richness of each other, they can blaze an unmarked trail together instead of continuing on their individual beaten paths.

Karen and Lucas did exactly that and now live the best of both worlds. The more they respected each other's differences and the less they insisted on their own views, the more they deepened their love and enriched their lives through compromise. They moved to a quiet small town in between the city and the country and Karen couldn't help but love the puppy Lucas brought home. Karen still does not play golf and Lucas still resents the idea of crowded beaches, but living close to the water, both cherish the nightly routine of walking their dog along the beach. In compromising you receive the best of each other and realize that there are just as many good qualities in the other person as there are in you.

   3.   Her daughter is running our relationship.

Should I wait until her daughter has grown out of it or should I leave the relationship? If you decide to wait, you may be waiting forever, but leaving someone you love and respect is also a rather dumb move. This is a temporary problem and will only become permanent if you avoid the issue or try to tackle it in the absence of *mutual respect*.

Susan and Ben have known each other for 2 years, are in love and are planning to get married. Ben harbors concerns about Allison, Susan's ten-year-old daughter from her previous marriage. A beautiful, bright and lively girl, Allison is indeed running their relationship as she engages in the controlling behavior of a victim. Her actions range from exhaustive attention seeking to complaining and manipulating to evoke guilt. Ben and Susan are living their lives according to the script of a frightened girl with an injured soul. Allison is threatened by Ben's presence and fears sharing or even losing her mother's love. Through manipulation, Allison tries to control the situation in order to minimize her fear and loss. As long as Susan participates in this struggle and Ben remains a passive bystander, the happiness of all is at stake. By respecting everyone's feelings this impediment can be resolved constructively. Allison, no longer the center of her mother's life, feels insecure and her fears need to be acknowledged and respected. Ben is not entirely powerless in this situation. He can support Susan in demanding Allison's respect not only for her mother, but also for Ben. Susan must recognize her guilt-driven acceptance of Allison's disrespectful behavior and claim her entitlement to happiness and love with Ben.

As parents we feel guilty about our shortcomings, divorce, material things we cannot afford for our children, putting our needs before theirs and spending too little time with them. We feel guilty when our children do not measure up in our social comparison, and in our guilt we often mentally cripple our children for life. Because of this guilt, we often fail to command respect from our children. Why do we buy these travel vouchers for guilt trips? Even if our own résumés lack credibility, our children are our social reference; we can rise through our children.

While it is true that our children will run this world some day, many children run their parents lives even before they can vote. Just as many parents do not command respect from their children, they also do not grant their children the respect they deserve. I am opposed to children running their parents' lives or relationships with manipulative games; I equally resist the idea that the needs and lives of children are less important than those of their parents. *Mutual respect* in parent/child or in any other relationship is very important. Neglecting to teach the principle of *mutual respect* fosters much of the emotional volatility, insecurity and low self-esteem in children. Susan and Ben resolved their problem by simply acknowledging its existence and presenting a united front to Allison.

Control

The real point is that if we truly love and are being loved, we respect and feel morally responsible to others. More precisely, we are interested in communicating our respect and obligation to those we love, however unskilled we may be at this task. With *mutual respect* and *moral responsibility* for one another, we no longer feel the need to lie, cheat, control, manipulate or disempower each other; we are able to create harmonious relationships without fear or emotional stress.

Even though it is simple to build meaningful relationships when they are based on the concepts of *mutual respect* and *moral responsibility*, such relationships are the exception rather than the rule. To believe in this concept beyond its theory might be difficult, because it challenges not only the rewards to which we believe ourselves entitled in our relationships, but also our conditional views on love.

Fearing vulnerability and dependency, we hesitate to completely commit in relationships. At the beginning of a new relationship we are so occupied with our own expectations that we fail to explore the entirety of the other person. At the same time we are so concerned with being lovable enough that we forget to be ourselves. We fear giving up independence, making the wrong love choices, and we are afraid of falling in love. Even when it is safe to open our hearts we are weakened by the anxiety that this love will disappear and fear the pain of potential abandonment.

When holding back intimacy, we claim to do so in order to protect our vulnerability; however, I strongly believe that the real reason lies in wanting to control the other person. As long as we withhold intimacy from someone who is ready to give it, the other will bend over backwards to achieve intimacy, giving us the power and control in the relationship.

Often we end relationships when it becomes apparent that it will take effort to resolve conflict. We no longer have the patience to allow anything worthwhile to progress. Our relationship attempts begin to resemble the McValue concept in the fast food industry: fast, cheap and easy, and unfortunately many of us turn into relationship jerks and junkies.

Meaningful relationships are developmental processes whereby intimacy grows through commitment. Without commitment, relationships have no purpose or staying power. Today we worship independence, individuality and control over others, and are often unable to create intimacy and commitment.

Unfortunately, in relationships, the presumptions of control and prediction are not applicable. Even though we can make an inference about its direction, we cannot predict or control the outcome of relationships. There is no blueprint for relationships and therefore our need to control remains dissatisfied. There are no guarantees in relationships or in life, but we do everything to seek security and are unwilling to live and love without guarantees.

It is my firm belief that it is not guarantees we seek, but control over events, people and outcomes. Somehow we have come to believe that controlling another leads to predictable love, an outcome less frightening than unpredictable love. By controlling the outcome of a relationship we try to guard ourselves against the pain of abandonment. In so doing, we sever ourselves from the flow of life and love.

Losing love and coping with the ensuing distress is certainly one detrimental outcome we seek to avoid at all costs. When a relationship ends and we still love the other person, the resulting pain often renders us powerless. We believed this love would last forever, but now we feel we are entering a dead end street as we imagine a bleak, loveless future. I believe that much of the pain we experience is due to our sudden loss of control. As long as we are with this person, we have some control over eliciting loving responses from our partner. Therefore, we can control the amount of love we need from the other in order to feel validated and loved. When the relationship is over, this well of energy dries up and our frame of reference changes. Our self-concept becomes negative and we no longer feel lovable and give our power away.

Maybe one or both of you were not ready for true love. Perhaps you needed to learn a lesson from each other and the lesson is over. You may have been hindering each other's personal growth. Whatever the reason, if the one you claim to love cannot be happy with you, how can you be happy with him or her? Forego seeking fault in yourself, for love has no reason. Love either is or is not. Instead of becoming angry and self-critical, realize that someone leaving you only means he or she has chosen to go on without you, not against you.

As paradoxical as it may sound, losing love can also be a positive experience. By allowing another to leave in love and wishing that person well, you develop your own ability to love further. Use the experience of lost love, no matter how painful, as a springboard for an even greater love. Keep your loving soul intact instead of reducing it through fear and anger. There is so much more love in your future because you have come closer to true love than ever before. Open up your soul and take the high road. This is the only way you can make sense out of being left by someone you wanted to be with.

In retrospect, my own experience has been that every time I suffered pain over lost love I survived and surfaced as a stronger, more humble person. I have learned that there is always more love after a relationship is over. Although my most salient lessons grew out of grief, my growth always came from someone who loved and believed in me. No matter how painful the journey, knowing that I could overcome being defeated by love has diminished my fear of dealing with death. Losing love has made me aware that nothing lasts forever, including me. Knowing that with such certainty, how dare I not embrace each moment with all the intensity it offers? How dare I not love as far as I can, and how dare I not make my relationship the best it can possibly be? Loving without fear eliminates your need to control those you love. In this sense, fearless loving is truly a triumph of love and life.

Most singles launch one meaningless relationship after

another and far too many settle into the glorified singlism. Such relationships may end for many valid reasons, including abuse, addiction, serious mental or emotional shortcomings or simply lack of deep feelings for the other. The commitment shyness that prevents many from experiencing intimacy is probably the main killer of relationships that otherwise have great potential. When only one partner is prepared to commit to greater intimacy or is on a different timetable this definitely creates conflict. The prospect of continuing the relationship fades when the conflict is avoided and commitment is not forthcoming. One person feels left in the dark and the other is being put on the spot. Typically these relationships end on one of the following notes:

- I thought I was in love, but I am not.
- Why do you need to know where this relationship is going?
- Can we not simply enjoy what we have?
- I am not sure if I am ready.

The reasons for commitment shyness are as diverse as relationships themselves, but I will discuss some of the main reasons. Confronted with the issue of commitment while still unsure of our feelings for the other person, we give the appearance of commitment until we are either sure or something better comes along. Reluctance to commit even when we feel deeply for a person arises out of fear of making the wrong choice. Which horse do we bet on among all the pretty horses? Many times it is not the wrong choices that lead to the cycle of multiple relationships and break-ups, but failure to make the choice to commit. Once commitment is established we can nurture our own horse into the most beautiful horse on the track.

My friend Kevin once told me the following:

Men are more reluctant to commit than women, because their fear of being taken advantage of emotionally and financially is greater than that of women. For men, being made a fool is a far greater concern than being taken for money because appearing a fool hurts their pride. Because the majority of men have a big ego, they need to know that a woman is crazy about them before they commit, even though being crazy about someone is not the same as being loved. The bigger a man's ego, the more it needs to be fed and the longer it takes for him to become committed. Most attractive people (men or women) have a bigger need to have their ego fed because they are accustomed to all the attention and are aware that they are in high demand. In truth, when constant validation has to come from outside sources, we are really talking about a weak ego. For many it would be more beneficial if they weren't so attractive, because they would actually be better human beings.

Many of us maintain meaningless relationships in which we distance ourselves emotionally from each other. One primary reason is that we try to manipulate our partners into what we need them to be. When our partners fail to become what we want, we become disillusioned with the relationship. Our partner no longer lives up to the image of the miraculous person with whom we thought love would last a lifetime. As a result, we wordlessly retreat from each another, withdraw intimacy and either openly or silently hold the other person responsible for not meeting our standards. In this distressing power struggle we drain each other's energies and rob one another of the quality of life. We either dwell in these relationships, playing out the continuous control dramas, or we plan to exit in our quest for a new love.

We are taught to watch out for ourselves first and are sold on the idea of getting the most out of life. This widespread "me first" attitude has made us somewhat insensitive to others. Time and again we measure the quality of our lives by how much we achieve or receive, and by how well our needs are met instead of by how much we contribute. In our self-absorbed thinking it is no surprise that we grow increasingly disrespectful and impatient towards the needs of those around us. Immersed in our own needs and what we perceive to be our rights, we turn a blind eye to many of our duties and obligations as human beings.

Disconnectedness has reached such an alarming degree that partners often no longer know each other's thoughts and feelings. In such circumstances people cohabit like strangers, experience loneliness and grow apart. We believe in the myth of independence telling us that the less we need someone and the more autonomous we are, the less vulnerable we are. This illusion produces a false security, widens the gap of emotional disengagement and leads us into relationships of interest rather than meaning. Relationships formed out of interest become dissatisfying, or deteriorate as soon as our interests change.

❤ Fear, a Life-Bandit

In truth, everything that you are, have been and will be, is because of your relationships with others.
—Professor Charles Levine (2001)

All meanings originate out of interactions with others. Terms such as "love," "happiness" or even "truth" are never just ideas, but meanings that arise from experience. The meaning we attribute to love is the result of sharing love with others. Love has no meaning outside of relationships and neither does anything else. We construct meaning out of every object, situation or person with whom we come into contact and these meanings become part of who we are. Our self-concept is constantly defined by the feedback we receive from others; we therefore cannot know ourselves outside of relationships. Whether our lives are meaningful is entirely dependent upon our cumulative relationships with all the people in our lives.

To illustrate this significance, just imagine yourself growing up on an island isolated from any human interaction. Disregard everything that you have learned and been exposed to and envision yourself as starting all over in isolation. To begin with, you would not learn a language and could not even think about yourself and the world you live in. In the absence of human interaction you would not be able to develop a self-concept because your identity is dependent on feedback from others. You could not distinguish between good and bad, joy and sorrow, right or wrong. We depend entirely on interaction with others to derive shared meanings of our identities and lives.

The whole notion of love is a shared meaning derived out of interactions with those we love, and if our relationships are meaningless so are our lives. Instead of creating meaning in a present relationship, many people *relation-hop* hoping to find the meaning of love in yet another relationship. In simple terms, the statement "I love you" has no meaning outside of a relationship.

In order to have loving relationships we need to depend on each other. Even if you consider yourself a self-made person, you will soon realize that no one achieves anything alone. As you remember those who assisted you in reaching your goals by paving the way, giving financial help or encouragement, you will appreciate the reality that we truly depend on each other. Once you understand that relationships can only be meaningful with *mutual respect* and *moral responsibility*, you can be a catalyst for world change instead of simply letting the world act upon you.

Many of us are paralyzed by the fear that our next experience with love will be a reflection of our past experiences and are unwilling to take a risk again. We have become judgmental about love because of what we have learned through past experience. This past creates tension or even unwillingness to learn something that contradicts our experiences. Moreover, adopting new beliefs necessitates re-thinking the self, which implies a threat to our ego. Fear is an emotion arising out of our perception as to what is a threat. Everything we think and do is influenced by our emotions, which explains how fear greatly influences our behavior.

We fear the beginning of a relationship as much as we fear the ending. This is evident in numerous people who fear not being loved as much as they fear being hurt by love. This fear of love is present in existing relationships as well as among singles, and deprives us of the experience of love. Many singles are afraid of spending their lives without someone who loves them in return. Those in relationships fear being left by the one who claims to love them. This fear prevents many from surrendering and creating a love that could last a lifetime.

People avoid conflict fearing the tension it creates and, out of fear of not being loved, they act out roles. For many in emotionally or physically abusive relationships, the fear of living with the abuser may be just as profound as the fear of living without. For singles, fear of loneliness is often the reason for entering into relationships prematurely. For others, the fear of growing old alone is so enormous that they will endure an established relationship even if the relationship proves to be unrewarding. Apart from those who claim to be voluntarily single, there are many who delay entering a relationship out of fear of getting hurt.

Let's get one thing straight. Love and life will never be without fear, and there is no absolutely fearless way to love or even live. We must distinguish between fear and anxiety even though both may feel the same. Fears are situational, of limited duration and help us avoid hazardous situations and risky decisions. It would be crazy, for instance, to stay in a swimming pool in the middle of a thunderstorm. This positive, commonsense fear is biologically based and serves to protect us from real danger. In contrast, there are non-situational, less imminent fears, such as the vision of your teenage daughter being in a traffic accident, failing an exam, embarrassment, rejection or being hurt in a relationship. These are negative fears pertaining to potential events. At their best, such non-situational or hypothetical fears are anxieties meant to caution us but, at their worst, they elicit fear of uncontrollable future events. Unfortunately these fears or anxieties interfere with our enjoyment of life, to the point of robbing us of many wonderful experiences.

Gregory's fear of dying in a plane crash caused him life-long anxiety and prevented him from visiting his son, daughter-in-law and grandchildren in Australia. Lack of money and time rarely permitted his son's family to visit Gregory. Since he was retired and in good health Gregory could have spent much treasured time in Australia with the only family he had left. He never watched his grandson play soccer or heard his granddaughter sing in the choir. Gregory's fear of flying was based on remote and speculative concerns. When his son and his entire family were killed in a car accident, Gregory did fly to attend their funeral in Australia and, for the first time, he saw the country they had called their home. Gregory left Australia mourning that he had not lived his life to the fullest and had not embraced life's dearest treasures: those he loved. His memory was filled with regret over all the happy smiles, loving moments and the precious miracles he could never savor. He had become a casualty of a fear that molded his life and he missed out on the true meaning of life. Unless our anxieties reach a degree of clinical dysfunction, we can manage them by simply paying attention to the positive fears that I mentioned before, and by using common sense. Gregory's flying anxiety was most likely due to his lack of control while on a plane. He felt most secure with both feet on the ground. Common sense could have told him that he would be safe in the hands of an experienced pilot.

Most of our anxieties arise out of our desire to control our lives and when we lose control our level of anxiety increases. "Love-fear" is an anxiety arising from being powerless in controlling those we love or their love for us. Even those who pledged marriage vows are often weighed down by the anxiety of losing love for one reason or another. If we believe love is something we either do or do not deserve, we feel obligated to do something to get it, and to do even more to hold on to love. With this conditional view of love, it is not surprising that we are so anxious about losing love should we fail to do that which elicits love from the other person.

Our self-esteem in relationships depends on whether we receive enough love as defined in our own terms, and we often try to manipulate our mates into loving us the way we see fit. Sometimes this manipulation reaches a point where no matter how much we love each other, we could never be successful in demonstrating our love. There is much advice available about how to get the love we want, leading us to believe that if we were only assertive enough we could have our wish-lists fulfilled. If we could free ourselves from the notion that love is about getting what we want, we could be liberated from our efforts to control. This control is precisely what obstructs the process of love. When love is tied to expectations, we manipulate our partner's role performance, which is often at variance with who they are. Role-manipulation presents the most serious limitation in relationships, because it undermines the authentic self, generates anxiety over role-expectations, and adds to our already present love-fear.

Love is also about overcoming the pain of the past, being who we are and developing our human potential. There should be an equal opportunity for each of us to reach our potential in a relationship; sometimes all it takes to succeed is someone who really loves us. Because of love-fear, far too many people feel threatened by their partner's growth and are afraid that their thriving partners no longer need them. Loving means recognizing the positive in your partner and helping him or her to become more of who he or she is.

I hope you realize that when you control or manipulate another, you are disrespectful and morally irresponsible, because you are playing with another person's emotions and mind. If this is all you ever take away from this book, I will be thrilled and so will you, because as you stop mind and control games your love-fear will disappear. You will no longer be afraid of losing love, and, maybe for the first time in your life, you will not only be loved for who you are but also for letting another person love as a free human being. In place of "I love you, if you love me first," try thinking, "I love you because of who I can become with you." In this sense love may be seen as a meaningful and purposeful interdependence through which we can become so much more than is possible on our own.

Many may feel challenged by the idea of equitable intimacy because many traditional gender stereotypes are still with us. Some men still need to have their ego stroked by their partners and like to maintain the upper hand in relationships. In this sense, equitable intimacy threatens many men and undermines the prospect of their getting away with controlling the relationship.

Women, on the other hand, who have historically been the losers in inequitable relationships, now seek autonomy and freedom from the demands of ego-centered men. However, many men are still reluctant to give up control. While women resent being controlled, they too engage in controlling behavior, however subtle it may be. In contrast, equitable relationships in which partners respect each other as human beings are built on trust and have a much greater survival rate because of this crucial backbone. Trust requires giving the other person freedom and space. If people are confined or imprisoned by control they will find a way out!

> *A woman marries a man expecting him to change and he doesn't. A man marries a woman expecting her not to change and she does.*
> —Author Unknown

What are the risks of giving up control and loving with all of our hearts? If you are a love "in-activist" who thinks about love, imagines being in love and has read almost everything on the subject, then you are theoretically prepared for love. However, as long as you have only a vision of love, you have nothing to fear until you move from thought into action. When you do, you become a love "activist" who either pursues love or is already in love. Once you understand *mutual respect* and *moral responsibility* you have nothing to fear. You throw your heart in front of you and try to catch it. You will know that love itself never hurts and that it unfolds no matter what you do. When you are afraid of being hurt by love, you fear that your love is not reciprocated or that this love will end. All these fears have one thing in common. They are solely about your own needs and have nothing to do with the other person. When you love someone for his or her own sake, you have nothing to fear and there are no limits to the way you can share your heart.

❤ Who Will Get a Clean Bill of Emotional Health?

The fact that we are preoccupied with our own needs in relationships has been mentioned throughout this book. The book market is literally flooded with recommendations on how to spot the right person and the characteristics he or she should possess. Given these guidelines, just about anyone should be able to generate an animated computer image of the right person. This abundant material is just as riddled with warnings about those who do not qualify as relationship material. Relationship texts routinely suggest ideal partners and recommend ideal types of relationships. In other words, perfect people will have perfect relationships. Whole sections are devoted to how to become the ideal mate in order to have an ideal relationship. Statements such as, "If you don't love yourself, nobody else will," make me wonder how much we have to love ourselves in order to be loved. The directive should be "If you don't respect yourself, nobody else will." As I have already stated, love is a process arising out of interactions with others and to love ourselves we need feedback from others.

I have tried some of the suggestions from personal-development and relationship-building books. One method suggested standing in front of the mirror and talking positively and encouragingly to yourself. As I stood there patting myself on the back I couldn't help feeling rather silly. Another technique advocated plastering mirrors and fridges with uplifting, affirmative messages so as to let the suggestive power of repetition take hold of my mind. Unfortunately, my daughter protested the lack of space on the fridge for shopping lists and school memos.

I take issue with our preoccupation with measuring up to the ideal psychological type, for the same reason as I take issue with measuring up to an ideal physical type. Far too many believe that they will miss out on love unless they pass an emotional health test defined by some authority. In chapter 2, I discussed Maslow and Rogers's definition of emotionally healthy individuals, and made the point that many put their lives on hold to reach this ideal state of emotional health.

Leading behavioral researchers concluded that almost 80 percent of our thoughts about others and ourselves are negative, rendering us unable to find peace within ourselves. In reading literature on emotional health that points out numerous characteristics commonly missing in us, I am not in the least surprised that more and more people feel emotionally inadequate or depressed. According to experts, the number of people displaying emotionally unhealthy approaches to life, or who are suffering from some form of mental illness, has risen from 10 percent to 20 percent since World War II. Ironically, this increase has paralleled the growth of the pharmaceutical industry, a billion dollar, ostensibly legitimate, business of *mind-warping*.

The 1999 publication of the Citizens Commission on Human Rights (CCHR) refers to the *Diagnostic Statistical Manual for Mental Disorders* (DSM), published by the American Psychiatric Association (APA). According to CCHR the number of recognized disorders in this mental-health bible has risen from 112 in 1952 to 374 in 1994. Classifications for mental disorders now include stuttering, spelling, mathematical and sibling rivalry disorders, all of which are used to label people in non-standard terms.

Have mind and behavior experts taken ordinary human imperfections and imaginatively converted them into mental confusions and disorders requiring extensive therapy or costly drugs in aid of the pharmaceutical industry? I really question whether the "discovery" of new psychological ailments is really helping us. On the contrary, I think they are making at least half of us feel inadequate and, as a result, many come to perceive themselves as mentally below par. Although serious mental illness does exist and some people display severely deficient coping skills, I challenge the allegation that so many of us have turned into less competent, more troubled humans.

I recently examined a so-called relationship kit (the book, the tapes, the quizzes, etc.) that very convincingly assures readers that true love is within the reach of us all. As I continued reading this promising text, an extensive section listed numerous characteristics and behavioral attitudes that disqualified most people as relationship material. According to this literature, a person is required to pass a clean bill of emotional health to participate in a relationship. This definition of an emotionally healthy person is based on the fabrication of an ideal person who certainly has no resemblance to anyone I have ever met. Moreover, it eliminates over 80 percent of the population as candidates for loving relationships.

It is common practice in the field of psychology, and in the relationship business, to over-analyze emotional health and encourage people to live up to some ideal. Many of our normal human moods and behaviors have been assigned arbitrary psychological terms. In fact, if you want to make something important out of something you don't understand, just see a psychologist. If he or she can't help, you may be referred to a psychiatrist; but keep in mind that if you see angels everywhere, you may be happier than your shrink.

You may also opt for cyber-therapy, the future remedy for those who need to be brought into alignment with the norm. Cyber-therapy can be an excellent and cost-efficient way to help those with seemingly unsolvable problems who would otherwise be excluded from the luxury of a practice visit. However, the imaginary cyber-couch is probably not always a bed of roses.

Recently my friends logged on to dream therapy with an accredited psychologist, and were asked to compose a dream journal. Their wild dreams are more amusing than they are reason for concern. After being prompted to click on several options to help describe their dreams, their dreams were interpreted as follows:

1. One of my friend's recurring dreams about being literally hit by hard cash all night was interpreted as a pending cash crisis, layoff from her job or someone getting ready to take her to the cleaners. The truth is that my friend believes that all it would take to cure her inability to balance her checkbook is a sizeable cash injection.

2. My teacher-friend was troubled by dreams about two of her third grade students dying horrific deaths. It was deduced that she was most likely not adept at classroom management, suffered from insecurities or was otherwise incompetent as an authority figure. Quite frankly, my friend was fed up with the behavior of these ill-mannered brats who terrorized the classroom.

Much counseling and therapy focuses on our alleged negative behavior to the point of making even ordinary responses to life look abnormal. Truthfully, most people are actually quite sane despite statistical results to the contrary. Erik Erikson, a social-psychologist who focuses on the formation of our identity (and who also makes the most sense to me), has suggested that an emotionally healthy person is one who possesses hope, will, purpose, competence, fidelity, love, care and wisdom.

These are also attributes of a person who under the influence of an optimal upbringing has developed a positive self-concept. I simply doubt that many of us have been subjected to ideal rearing. As a result most are not in this so-called ideal emotional state. Against the backdrop of a less than optimum upbringing, are we emotionally healthy enough to give and receive love or are we destined to do without? While we are unable to re-invent our childhoods, we are still very capable of looking at ourselves differently, and realizing that almost nobody matches the ideal of an emotionally healthy person. This realization alone can make us feel a lot more "normal."

As we are trying to live up to the ideal, chained by our past, we skip over love and life itself. If most of us are supposedly not emotionally healthy due to less than perfect childhoods, what then is an appropriate non-academic definition of an emotionally healthy person? I suggest the simplest definition would include a truth-seeking, truth-speaking and truth-living individual of integrity. The fact that each of us perceives his or her world from a different perspective accounts for many different truths, and truth itself, again, is a process arising out of interaction with others.

This brings us back to the importance of relationships. Without relationships, you can never discover the truth about yourself. All of us are capable of seeking, defending and living our own truth as much as we are capable of respecting the truth of others. Unfortunately, we are programmed to do the exact opposite. Instead of being truthful about ourselves, we believe that the truth about us is never adequate or good enough. As a result, we feel compelled to present a "better us" in order to be accepted.

❤ Why We Feel Inadequate

Most of us live in disguise, withholding our true self in favor of a fabricated self we believe to be more acceptable. We are constantly fed by a multitude of influences reassuring us that we are not good enough in more ways than one. We are not smart enough, not rich enough, not skinny enough, not efficient enough, not pretty enough, not powerful enough, not resourceful enough, not "with it" enough, and probably out of it all together.

By judging each other and ourselves we reinforce the beliefs that we are not good enough. The dividing line between humans has become one of comparison and competition for the best seats in the house. To feel superior we need to look for someone we believe to be inferior. This reckless competition ensures that we stay motivated enough to become everything that we are not.

In our senseless participation in the rat race, we give up our identities to those who mold and shape us; we are no longer vitally involved in the formation of our own identities. We go through life, threatened by faster and better rats, and in the end we feel that the "winners took it all." Unfortunately most of us cannot win the game, break even or quit. Comparing ourselves to others undermines our own self-worth, devalues our abilities and conceals our own truth. As we allow others to define us we become a nation of weak egos unable to know and defend ourselves. If all we ever aim for is to seek, speak, defend and live our truth, we will become emotionally healthy and respectfully accept our genuine self.

1. Seeking your truth

The belief that you are not good enough is a reflection of how others have labeled you. When you accept these labels you live your life according to them. Like most people, you use much of your energy living up to positive labels and taking corrective steps to repair negative labels.

For example, for the longest time I was labeled dumb and somewhat useless and wholeheartedly believed in these labels and acted accordingly. I failed at school, misbehaved, sought trouble, and truly succeeded in living up to the image of a dumb and useless person. I spent much of my life suspicious of my own judgment but never doubted the judgment of those around me. Eventually, I realized that behind all these negative labels had always been a bright and intelligent person. I had given my power to my judges and never allowed the true me to unfold.

In this example you can replace the words "dumb" and "useless" for any other negative properties you have come to believe about yourself. Underneath all your negative beliefs is a very capable, unique and perfect human being, responsible for seeking the truth about yourself instead of subscribing to the verdicts of others. There is nobody who knows you better than yourself, no better authority to consult than you, and no better judgment than yours.

Do not fear who you are, as the truth about yourself is truly the best of you. By seeking your truth and re-claiming yourself, you focus your energy on the best in you, instead of wasting your efforts on disabling labels that are only the perceptions of others. The decision about who you are is too important to leave to others and as long as you are able to think, you can change your thoughts about yourself. Deep down you have a vision of who you are, and when you trust this vision you will embrace yourself. You will find love by releasing the best part of you: your humble and unpretentious self. Seeking your truth is the first step in becoming emotionally healthy.

You are here to figure out who you are and what you are supposed to do and then do it.
—BEVERLY WILKINS

2. Speaking your truth

As you discover your truth you will stop lying to yourself and build confidence in yourself. You no longer have to be what others expect you to be and do what you don't want to do. The need to pretend, to self-promote, to impress and to say things you either don't mean or don't believe in will disappear. You understand that the negative things you believed about yourself were simply the thoughts of others and you will stop beating yourself up. As you develop a sense of self, you trust your instincts, are prepared to act on them, respect yourself and others and, in the process, you gain an open mind. With this open mind you realize you have just as many beliefs as you have disbeliefs. Nothing ever "just is," and sometimes what is true today may no longer be true tomorrow. You are someone who knows some things, but who you are is not tied to this knowledge. You are no longer ambiguous about who you are. It is no longer important to be right, as your ego is no longer tied to your knowledge.

You stop making assumptions about others and no longer label them. Instead you engage in honest dialogues and respect that the world is full of listeners and speakers who, driven by standards and fears, are also unable to express their truth. You realize that all people have a right to speak and that you have an obligation to listen and that each opinion, view or belief is as important as yours. When you speak your truth you'll want to watch your words, because you may have to eat them later. You will use compassionate language when you speak about others and yourself, and will represent the true you with dignity. When you listen to people, you do so with respect for their views and when you speak about others you do so with kindness. As your thoughts change, your language becomes humane and your loving words reach others. Through your benevolent speech you create a peaceful, safe and fearless environment for everyone you encounter and choose meaningful experiences with others.

3. Living your truth

You are somebody important and you do matter (if you think not, try missing a car payment). You discover that your greatest privilege as a human being is to use your abundance of love and your capacity to love all there is. You no longer do less than what you are capable of and, instead, use all your God-given abilities. By giving your best to those around you, you prompt people to give their best. You treat people with love and bring out their most loving ways. You treat people with trust and they will not betray you. You treat people with honesty and make your presence a safe place for them. You trust your abilities and along the way teach others to trust theirs. You do the right thing even when you do not receive recognition. You treat people with kindness and receive kindness in return. You keep the faith even when encountering defeat, and you stand tall in the face of adversity. Your heart has no room for hate, which destroys the spirit like malignant cells, for you know that there is so much more power in love. Your thoughts create your perception of your world and you are entirely responsible for everything that you choose to think. By choosing positive, loving thoughts you believe in people and, hopefully, trust in God.

Most of us do not need professional help to achieve emotional health. We can achieve emotional health by simply finding and living our truth. By honoring ourselves, we illuminate our paramount person, trust our purpose and find acceptance and love. Having love in your life makes up for many things you don't have, and makes you feel complete as it fills the emptiness in your heart. Chances are that when you have love, you will never need a psychiatrist.

Never forget that a half truth is a whole lie.
—AUTHOR UNKNOWN

❤ 5 Principles to Remember from Chapter Seven

1. *Mutual respect* is an imperative building block of any healthy relationship.
2. We fear not being loved, just as much as we fear being hurt by love.
3. Your relationships with others create everything that you are and always will be.
4. We control and manipulate our partners into loving us the way we see fit.
5. If you have love, chances are you'll never need a psychiatrist.

CHAPTER 8

WE WERE BORN NAKED, WET AND HUNGRY AND THEN IT GOT WORSE
There Is No Reality, Only Perception

> *When "Do no evil" has been understood, then learn the harder, braver rule, "Do good."*
> —ARTHUR GUTTERMAN (1871–1943)

MOST PEOPLE ASSUME that the condition of their relationship is due to a combination of the upbringing and the psychological state of each person involved. There is much to be learned about how present social environments shape not only individuals but also entire relationships. Imagine two people of fairly similar socio-economic backgrounds and similar upbringing living in a rural village. As their relationship unfolds in a rural environment their issues will be quite different than those they would face if they lived in the city.

In reality, we all change through our human interactions and continually altering environments. In other words, who we are depends to a great degree on the environment in which we live or work. A specific behavior of our partner may never have revealed itself if he or she had not been exposed to a particular setting. The environments to which our relationships are subjected determine many of the problems we face and how we deal with them. Often we do not take circumstances such as work conditions, living arrangements, financial issues, interfering relatives or draining friends into account, and we look for the cause of relationship problems solely in our partners. Many people go around in circles trying to solve their problems, but fail to acknowledge the circumstances outside the relationship that either contribute to the problem or cause it altogether. Often when outside factors are considered and dealt with, the entire relationship improves.

Sharon and Kent experienced friction when his mother openly expressed dislike for Sharon. Even though he was aware of his mother's behavior, Kent did not demand respect for the wife he loved. Instead, he tacitly condoned his mother's disrespect hoping that Sharon would ignore a situation that would disappear on its own. Indirectly he accorded less respect to Sharon than to his mother. For Sharon, this caving-in meant a denial of her self-respect as well as her authentic self. Once Sharon saw how this outside influence threatened their union, she demanded respect from both Kent and his mother. As Sharon stood up for herself, Kent realized that their problems had begun when they moved closer to his mother. He acknowledged that they either needed to distance themselves from his mother's influence or his mother had to change her attitude. Sharon also knew that her only chance to gain respect was to live her own truth in kindness. In reality, we teach others how to treat us, and by allowing others to treat us disrespectfully, we teach them that we are not worthy of respect.

In the above example, it becomes clear that situational constraints burdening a relationship need to be addressed or an otherwise gratifying relationship may be at stake. Once Sharon and Kent acknowledged their problem, they dealt with the issue head-on. Regardless how Kent's mother felt about Sharon, eventually she had to respect Sharon in order to remain in her son's life. Kent and Sharon are much happier now. Ironically, as Kent's mother changed her behavior, her attitude towards Sharon changed as well, and she couldn't help but begin to like her. Kent's mother had believed that daughters-in-law cause problems, take sons away and don't look after them as well as mothers. This generalized and harmful belief led to a negatively charged relationship between the two women. Often our dogmatic or pessimistic view of others prevents us from experiencing many of their remarkable qualities.

❤ It Is As Bad As You Think It Is and They Are out to Get You

Do you accept the spiritual (Creationism) or scientific explanation (Big Bang Theory and evolution) of how your world was created as true? The Big Bang Theory, the dominant scientific theory, states that the universe emerged through a random cosmic explosion. However, it does not explain where the matter came from and what caused its release. Maybe God was the creator of all matter in the first place. Science has compiled tremendous evidence in support of the Darwinian theory of evolution (evolution is the change in the gene pool of a population over time). Maybe God set the evolution process in motion.

Prior to the rise of science people accepted God's orchestration of humanity, but with the advent of science, empirical evidence has defined most of human nature and behavior. Whether you subscribe to Creationism or scientific explanation of the universe and human nature, one theory need not exclude the other or even prove the other wrong.

I often question the benefits of science as a whole: Have scientists really created better lives for us in their laboratories? It appears that our essential needs are to obtain connectivity, functioning families, clean water, fresh air, serenity, wholesome food, unconditional loving and peace of mind. We are threatened by terrorism. World peace is at stake and we still have not learned how to share our planet. The distribution of world resources is still imbalanced and western industrialized nations, representing merely 19 percent of the world's population, run the show for everyone. From unimaginable corporate fraud to untrustworthy politicians everywhere, we have seen it all. Is this the human nature we bought into? Maybe there is another human nature, evident in the fact that most ordinary people would rather be less greedy and share resources in favor of world peace and a re-emergence of integrity. Most people who believe in the goodness of human nature, and therefore the possibility of a better world, also believe in a greater spiritual being or a God. Most of us use science to acquire knowledge about human nature, but rely on religion as an insurance policy in the event that science has gone beyond discovery and actually shaped human nature.

To discover human nature, science observes thousands of rats of all shapes and sizes running mazes, chasing after food pellets or receiving shocks. Injected with hormones, these rats demonstrate that increased levels of testosterone are associated with aggressive behavior, suggesting this must be true of humans. Even though the nervous systems of non-human animals might be similar to those of humans, their brains and behavior certainly are not. Research of this type is conducted within a set stage and defined situation that triggers a certain behavior and is of an experimental nature, rather than an observational one.

Even if researchers observe humans or non-humans in their natural settings, the behavior elicited through the situational constraints may well be typical behavior unique to this specific environment but not necessarily representative of human nature. Human nature is as much situational or sociologically based as it is psychological, and our environments significantly shape our thoughts as well as our resulting behavior. Research conducted with non-rational animals has made claims about human nature depicting us as selfish, competitive, dishonest and hedonistic. Science has told us who we are and how we should live, but has left morality and certainly spirituality out of the equation.

We are indeed a species with the ability to reason, but may be hard-pressed to implement morality and integrity when human nature is seen as competitive, exploitative and self-indulgent. Competition is valued as an important characteristic and is the driving force that maintains our economic system. Employment seekers compete in a scarce labor market, people of color compete with Caucasians and women compete with men. Children learn early to compete with one another, young women compete at beauty pageants, businesses compete for market shares and countries compete for resources. We compete in an entirely arbitrary fashion and have accepted this competition as human nature. Those who do not or are unable to compete are more than willing to accept their lot since the seductive and widely established concept of the survival of the fittest is seen as human nature.

Are we genetically predisposed to be competitive, self-interested, uncaring, hedonistic and easily conditioned through rewards and punishment? Some scientists suggest that certain races are pre-disposed to less intelligence. Are some people biologically determined to live in famine and others are destined for fame? If it is human nature to strive excessively for material possessions, then are those in underdeveloped countries missing this competitive gene altogether?

We use a variety of explanations for human nature in our efforts to insure the survival of the fittest, and have come to see our competitive and narcissistic lifestyle as a the natural way of living. We are adamant about the biological basis for human nature and are convinced that we are unable to change it.

What is this thing called "human nature?" I mentioned in chapter 7 that leading behavioral research concluded that 80 percent of what we think is negative; therefore it stands to reason that 80 percent of what we think about our fellow humans is also negative. We seem to be occupied with putting most people down and letting the so-called fittest rise in our esteem and to the desirable places at the top of society.

Looking back over my life, those who stirred my soul were not necessarily the individuals with high IQs, nor were they the rich, sophisticated, educated and powerful whom I encountered *ad nauseam*. They were the loving, caring, humble and grateful people who encouraged me to open my heart, accepted me for who I was and made me laugh.

Just as there is no reality, only perception, so truth is never absolute or universal and there are many different truths of human nature. The answer to whether people are inherently good or bad is simply that they are both, depending on the situation or who is doing the judging. Whenever people are capable of something they are also capable of the opposite. Someone who lies is also capable of telling the truth. Someone who is intentionally uncaring is capable of caring. Someone who hates is also capable of loving. If you harbor negative perceptions about your fellow human beings and your relationships with others, then your romantic relationships will be negatively charged; and your partner will have to put exhaustive effort into convincing you that his or her human nature is good.

Who you have been, are now or ever will be is because of your relationships with others. This point was driven home in the previous chapter, but it needs to be stressed again: our relationships had better be of meaning for our lives to be meaningful. When you see the world occupied by mostly dreadful people who cannot be trusted your interactions become meaningless.

When you believe that people are bad by nature and analyze broken relationships you become convinced that what you believe about human nature is true. Rarely do you become reflexively aware of why you think what you think and whether what you think is even true. For this reason, most of us need to improve our thinking skills.

❤ It Is Entirely Their Fault

Do you believe everyone is out to get you, take advantage of you and play games with your mind? Do you expect the worst of people and relationships instead of the best? Do you feel that you constantly cast your pearls before swine? It is amazing how many of us blame others for relationships that did not last, for our inability to find a partner or for a current dissatisfying union.

> *My world is all right. I just don't know how all the other people fit in it.*
> —AUTHOR UNKNOWN

Every relationship that turned sour may not have been what you deserved, but it was exactly what you were asking for. You never asked for the now ex-wife who had an affair with your best friend or your little son Gary, who is not your son after all. Just like you never asked for that boyfriend who was unable to help you financially through tough times, but always had plenty of money to support his other girlfriend. Most people do not do those things if they are in relationships in which they feel safe, respected and closely connected. However, they may do such things if they are being controlled, manipulated or disrespected. Some may do those things if they feel insecure, have a weak ego or are in a relationship without support and encouragement.

Others will do those things because they believe it is human nature. Most would never do such things if they felt morally responsible and respected the other person and themselves.

All of us envision relationships in which we do not fight, lie, betray or control and simply love each other. We want these ideal relationships with our lovers, spouses, children, parents and relatives, but our belief that human nature is hedonistic and self-centered does not help us achieve these relationships. We must seriously ask ourselves who actually benefits from this negative thinking about human nature. In our pessimistic perception of humans, it is easy to see others as enemies, life as a warzone, and relationships as battlefields.

A coward is incapable of exhibiting love; it is the prerogative of the brave.
—MAHATMA GANDHI

Steve was devastated when he learned that Anita had used up their line of credit and maxed-out their credit cards. He had been so proud of her ability to dress stunningly and to decorate their house distinctively with (what Anita referred to as) bargain buys. Now the damage was done and Steve felt totally deceived. Even though he did not deserve it, could it be that he was setting the stage for mountains of debts? To some degree he was indeed inviting trouble. It was very important to Steve that Anita looked like a knockout, and that their home resembled a showpiece. Anita, who had low self-esteem to begin with, believed she would only be loved if she fulfilled Steve's expectations in both departments. Everywhere they went Steve's eyes constantly scanned other women, which over time sent Anita's self-esteem down the drain. The chore of keeping up her appearance became even more stressful when she showed signs of aging and weight gain. Anita invested heavily in dieting, age-defying products and a whole new wardrobe, all with the aim of hiding the extra pounds. She was acting disrespectfully and irresponsibly by putting their financial security at risk, while trying to do her best. Given that their relationship was built upon superficiality and revolved around trivial issues, Steve and Anita were not intimately connected nor did they truly love each other in a supportive way. Their relationship did not weather the burden of heavy debts and was destined to shatter.

Eventually, Anita fell in love with someone who loved and respected her, and as a result she blossomed in the face of true love. Steve continued to look for perfect bodies, ageless faces and other superficial traits without ever learning the lesson. Five years later, Steve lost his business and Anita's partner died in the line of duty. Soon thereafter Steve and Anita reunited as changed people. He had learned from disaster while she had grown through happiness. This time they knew that by implementing *mutual respect* and *moral responsibility* their relationship would not only survive, but also become rewarding.

In the final analysis of our lives there will never be anything that matters more than our relationships with one another. There will never be anything more meaningful than love. When you face disaster or even your own mortality and wind back the movie of your life, you will regret not having had the courage to love unconditionally. If you could live your life over again you would do everything on earth to be loved for your humble self. You thought you were on the right track and got run over. You intended to love all your life but never surrendered to it.

In our self-indulgent and self-absorbed way of living, the "I" and "me" have become more important than the "we." In a culture that portrays humans as innately selfish and endorses egotistical behavior, it seems difficult to envision people otherwise.

It raises the question as to whether the prevailing attitude of careless self-indulgence is a characteristic of individuals or a characteristic of our collective "me first" society. Curiously, while the "me first" attitude is typical of Western advanced industrialized societies, a very different human nature can be found in underdeveloped parts of the world.

As suggested before, people can be good or bad depending on their environment, but most are decent human beings. They do care, trust, step out of their way, love, give, support and make a difference, if we only let them.

While we are unable to change our society overnight, we are able to think differently about others, beginning with our own relationships. How dare we stop caring when there is so much left to care for! Just like you, most of us want to care and be cared for. From here on we need to treat each other with *mutual respect* and *moral responsibility* in our relationships if we are to reach human fulfillment. Not only are we capable of truly connecting with those we love but also with the rest of humankind. To bridge the gap between humans we must update our cognitive systems, improve our poor thinking skills, repair our defective communication and stop our unyielding assumptions about what we think is true of human nature. If we fail to do so, we will never understand how our thoughts, communication and assumptions have damaged our past relationships and continue to set the stage for the future.

❤ **Thinking:** *No matter how thin you slice it, there are always two sides.*

You are who you think you are. Others are who you think they are. The world is what you think it is, even if your thoughts are not true. When we strongly believe something, the facts rarely matter. We believe blindly in many ideologies that we accept as fundamental knowledge, even if there is evidence to the contrary or the circumstances change.

For example, my father's world has changed from horse-drawn buggies, to automobiles, to planes and nuclear warfare. He has witnessed an agricultural society change to an industrial one, and he remains left in the dark by the computer age. Throughout all these changes my father still believes Hitler did a great job cleaning up Germany, just as he still believes that people of color are inferior. John believes that people kill people and Anne believes that guns kill people. Barbara believes in life after death and Bob doesn't even believe in life after dinner. Ryan believes that marriage is a useless ordeal, while Leslie believes it to be essential. George believes that organically grown foods prevent diseases while Alice believes it does not matter what we eat, sooner or later we die anyway.

Beliefs about the same things can be as diverse as people themselves, and because we rarely think about our beliefs, we seek self-serving evidence in their support; beliefs such as:

1. It is obvious that people of color are less intelligent than white people. Why else do whites mainly occupy intellectually challenging positions? *(Could it not be that, due to racism still being very much alive, people of color have restricted access to those positions?)*

2. It is illogical to get married, if more than one out of two marriages fail. *(Is it not more reasonable to think that there is nothing wrong with the institution of marriage, but that there may be something wrong with the people joined in it?)*

Many of us cling to our beliefs for dear life, no matter how much information there is to the contrary. Because of our closed-mindedness we preserve our beliefs, never questioning how we arrived at them or whether they are even true. Considerable friction can be generated in relationships when two people defend opposing beliefs without considering the other person's point of view; just as many relationships never take off for the same reason.

Garret, a successful entrepreneur, did his utmost to convince Theresa that capitalism is the only economic system that provides equal opportunity. Theresa, a social worker, believes that capitalism is inherently wrong because someone's gain always seems to be someone else's loss. Garret, convinced his view is right saw no need to consider Theresa's opinion. While capitalism had worked for him, Theresa had seen the other side of the coin. Eventually he became so frustrated that he decided she was a communist bent on stealing from the rich to give to the poor. He believed his view to be superior and defended it in the absence of all the facts. As much as he loved Theresa, he ended this relationship because he foresaw problems arising from their opposing views. Neither Theresa nor Garret was right or wrong in their views, and the dissolution of their union was the result of poor thinking.

Most of us are guilty of being trapped in this type of unconstructive thinking. Even when we do not know the answer to many issues in life, we still defend our position even though we have given the issue only subjective thoughts. Who could ever know whether capitalism or any other economic system is best for a country?

Jane despised the welfare system until she needed it. Peter believed that Lisa's friends were uncultivated *low-lifes* until they became his steady anchor in a crisis. Many of our views are rather biased, in that we defend them as long as they serve our present needs and circumstances. Much of our faulty thinking comes from our subjective perception and leads to many unnecessary disagreements in relationships. In our fight for and over our beliefs, we break up relationships and even create enemies. Much of our thinking rotates around how convincingly we can defend our views; admitting that we are wrong is seen as a sign of weakness. If we are to have respectful, meaningful relationships, we must respect our partner's view in the same way as we respect our own. As long as we don't know for sure who is right or wrong we must continue to talk to each other and at least agree to disagree. There are at least two sides to an issue and only through dialogue can we ever get closer to the truth. The next time you argue with someone, disregard someone or even end a relationship over opposing beliefs, think about whether you know for sure that the position you defend is really right. When you recognize that the other person may be just as right or wrong as you are, you will discover your authentic intelligence of thinking.

❤ **Communicating:** *I am listening, but I can't hear you.*

Communication is the transmission of thoughts, feelings, and meanings among us, and can take place both verbally and non-verbally. Communication can be very complex. Communication errors in relationships are largely due to poor listening skills. Without listening, communication is impossible, but contrary to popular belief, listening is not an art. As long as you have functioning ears and are equipped with a standard brain you can master listening, if you care to.

Unless we listen closely and hear what the other person is saying, any verbal feedback we give is nothing more than a polite response. The main reason why we do not hear is because of our poor thinking skills. Most people think that what they have to say is more important, more interesting and more valid than the words of others. As long as we regard the words of others as less important, we will lag miles behind the essence of meaningful communication. With poor thinking skills, debates between people who love and value each other do not generate constructive solutions. Everyone appreciates the courtesy and respect of being listened to, particularly those we love and care about. As much as we insist that we are indeed listening, we are often not hearing. We interrupt by giving advice, finishing people's sentences and pronouncing what we believe the other person is about to say. Moreover, our minds are so busy lining up our own responses that we can't possibly hear the other person's words.

Pretending to listen and actually hearing are two different things. Hearing requires that we hold our tongue, allow speakers to finish and reply to what has been said. Hearing is much more than simply listening to words. It is the act of understanding the true meaning of what is said and respecting the speaker's feelings. Unfortunately, most of the time we allow our minds to gallop through the words without really hearing. We also lose sight of the fact that others don't always say what they mean, because they are either unskilled in expressing themselves or do not feel safe in stating their concerns.

Robert asked Jane for a weekend date. Jane responded: "Unfortunately I have already made plans for this weekend, which I cannot cancel." Robert inferred that Jane was not interested in him and left it at that. Because he did not ask for a subsequent date, Jane, very interested in Robert, assumed that he was not interested in her. The problem with this type of evasive communication is that neither said what they really meant and both failed to address the issue. The issue was not the weekend date, but rather was to determine if there was interest on either side. Fear of rejection and appearing a fool prevented both from discovering how they really felt. Robert could have asked her if she would be interested in a date for the following weekend. Jane could have said that even though she was tied up this weekend, she would be free the next weekend. Luckily, Jane did call Robert a few days later and they have been dating ever since. To really hear we must understand the meaning, by either re-phrasing what has been said or by simply asking, "What do you mean by that?" In Robert's case, he could have asked: "Would you like to go out another weekend?"

Establishing the meaning of what another is saying becomes much easier if you forget many of the rules about what to say when dating or in a relationship. When you hear from a place of kindness and humility you can say almost anything and ask non-accusing questions confidently. Questions such as "What exactly do you mean by that?" or " Do you mean . . . ?" and statements like "I am not sure I understand what you mean," become a natural tool in accurately understanding each other. Sadly, many believe that asking questions makes them appear unintelligent, even though the opposite is true. When we ask questions to clarify meanings, we express a sincere interest. We demonstrate that we care enough to really want to hear the meaning behind the words.

If we believe our words or feelings are more fascinating and important than those of anyone else, listening becomes an act of hypocrisy. With the focus on ourselves instead of the speaker it becomes rather obvious why we do not know how to "shut-up and listen."

In conversation, most of us, men and women alike, have the habit of "one-upping" others with a more dramatic story, or even hurting their feelings at a time when all they want is to be heard. In the singles world, I have repeatedly observed people struggling to become acquainted in conversation. Often one person talks non-stop about him- or herself, while the other person pretends to listen, showing only token head-nodding. Needless to say, in these encounters no real communication takes place, since the participants rarely remember more than the other's appearance. The non-stop speaker obviously has no clue about the listener. I am convinced that much would be gained if we trained ourselves to ask questions and really listened with all our hearts, in full attention. Asking genuine questions facilitates spontaneous interactions of natural flow, be they with a new encounter or a longtime partner.

As a writer you can imagine how I could "talk your ear off," if you cared to listen. However, I have had to teach myself to shut up and ask questions, because I would talk too much, sometimes to break the silence, other times to deal with anxiety or to control the conversation. In the end, I realized, that I knew nothing about the other person and was even challenged to remember their name. I might have been listening, but I did not ask any questions and I certainly did not hear anything. Since then I have become aware of my bad habit and realized that few care about how much I know or talk, they only care about how much I care. Now, I let people talk while I ask questions to clarify the meaning, and this has become the most exciting adventure for me. When I listen to others sharing their whole life stories, dreams, hopes, beliefs, opinions and expectations, I learn how precious and unique people really are.

We all need someone to listen to us at the best of times. When we are upset or confused we need the caring ears of our spouses, partners, friends or relatives. However, if we do not hear our partners' words we are unaware of what they think or feel. How will we ever get to know our partners if we do not listen? How could we ever truly love another human being without knowing his or her whole being? It is impossible to be connected with another person without listening, hearing and understanding.

Melinda discusses the latest home decorating ideas with her friend, while her husband feels devastated over the potential layoffs by his employer. Does this make sense?

If the people in your life are valuable to you (I told you that nothing will ever have more value than those you love), you will watch less TV, read fewer newspapers, stop spending hours on the Internet, stop chasing after perfection, worry less about a spotless house, the weeds in the garden, your hair, your looks and many other unimportant things. You will, however spend time getting to know those you love. You will ask questions, hear and respect their words. If you want to talk, you will wait for your turn. Hearing is like a strainer, the bigger the holes, the more stuff slips through. Make sure you holes are small so you won't miss the important words. It has been said that we were given two ears and one mouth, so we could hear twice as much as we talk.

Maybe one of the reasons why people talk to God is that He has no holes at all, never interrupts, does not give unsolicited advice, does not assume anything, asks many questions and He really hears.

IF I HAD MY LIFE TO LIVE OVER

I would have talked less and listened more. I would have invited friends over even if the carpet was stained and the sofa faded.
I would have taken the time to listen to my grandfather ramble about his youth.
I would have cried and laughed less while watching TV and more while watching life.
I would have shared more of the responsibility carried by my husband.

> *There would have been more I love yous... more I'm sorrys...*
> *but mostly, given another shot at life, I would seize every minute . . . look at it and really see it . . . live it . . . and never give it back.*
> —Erma Bombeck *(who lost her fight with cancer)*

❤ **Assuming:** *I know so much less than there is to know.*

At the grocery store check out, an old man in front of me experienced difficulties with his debit card. As he delayed a sizeable line-up, I overheard comments from those in line behind us: "If he has no money in his account, he shouldn't go shopping," "Maybe he stole the card," "He probably has dementia and can't remember his own pin number." Impatient people assumed all sorts of things about this old gentleman, who tried to apologize in a faint voice that could hardly be heard. After watching this embarrassed old man unsuccessfully trying to use his debit card, it became apparent that the debit machine was out of service.

Lester assumed that Kendra was upset when he watched a lot of sports on TV. After all, he had often heard about women's negative attitudes towards men who are occupied with TV sports. However, he did not want to miss the hockey season and told Kendra that he was helping a friend re-do his kitchen. Needless to say, there was little work done on the friend's kitchen during hockey season. Whenever Kendra would ask how the kitchen was coming along, Lester replied, "It is taking shape." The real point was that he assumed Kendra did not respect his hockey interest and so he hid his passion. Kendra, on the other hand, did understand his interest and wanted to spend time with him during hockey season. It appears that Lester should have asked instead of assuming, and a compromise could have been reached instead of seeking a safe haven in someone else's kitchen.

After dinner Julia enjoys a two-hour walk with her girlfriend, while Charles tends to office work or watches TV. When she started her walking regime, she asked Charles to join her, but he declined. Therefore, Julia assumed that Charles was not keen on walking and proceeded without him. After that, Julia walked five evenings a week and assumed that Charles kept himself occupied with what he wanted to do. Charles assumed that she preferred walking with her girlfriend and had difficulty understanding why Julia spent most evenings without him. In truth, Charles would have enjoyed walking with her some of the time, although maybe not for two hours almost every night. Julia would have loved walking with Charles, and contrary to what Charles assumed, she does not prefer to walk with her friend. The obvious conclusion is that wrong assumptions can lead to unfortunate misunderstandings in relationships.

We make assumptions about every imaginable situation or behavior, because of our need for immediate explanations for why people do or don't do things. We even go as far as assuming we know how people feel, what they think and predict what they will do. These assumptions are often made without the other person's input and represent one of the most dangerous forms of self-deception in relationships. In making assumptions about people, we assign motivations to their feelings and behavior without their consent. Assuming is dangerous, because we deceive ourselves as to the real reasons why people do or say something without verifying our assumptions. We often claim to know a person based on what we assume, and are surprised if they behave differently than expected.

Knowing that Rick is very shy in public, everyone was ready to bet money that Rick would never give a speech at Ashley's wedding. Luckily they didn't bet their life savings, because Rick walked in and delivered a well-prepared speech.

"My wife would never be caught dead in a country and western bar," said Woody, moments before her co-worker showed him pictures of his wife in western gear swinging on the dance floor.

Murray thought his wife would break down and be devastated when she learned about his affair, but that she would never leave him. She did find out. She did not break down and was not devastated; however, she did leave, took the kids and more than half the assets with her.

Let me assure you, the person you make assumptions about is the only one who knows how he or she feels and why he or she does one thing and not another. Just as you are the only one who knows your mind. What goes on in your mind is inaccessible to others, and that is why you must stop relying on assumptions about others, because more often than not they are misleading. Apart from emphasizing the importance of verifying your assumptions, I would like to remind you of the significance of asking questions and listening as discussed previously. Questioning and listening are the most critical tools in truly getting to know another person.

❤ 5 Principles to Remember from Chapter Eight

1. Science has shaped human nature more than it has discovered it.
2. What you believe about another person determines the type of relationship you will have.
3. When you strongly believe something, the facts rarely matter.
4. We assume so much about others and know so little.
5. There will never be anything more important than love.

CHAPTER 9

SEX VERSUS MAKING LOVE
From Failing Hard Drives to Silicone Floating Devices

> *Let there be sex at the end of the tunnel!*
> *I don't care about the light.*
> —Author Unknown

NO RELATIONSHIP BOOK could ever be complete without exploring the topic of sex, and no generation before us ever had such inexhaustible and even ruthless exposure to the minutest details of sex as we do. Our sex lives are attacked mercilessly for their inadequacy and failure to comply with current standards of sexual techniques. We have heard it all. From *Cosmopolitan's* 100 ways to achieve orgasm right down to libido increasing foods, erection extenders and premature ejaculation prevention. Our sex lives seem to require technical updates, like computer operating systems, but when pushing the start button many face system failures.

❤ Turning Our Lives Over to Hormones

Confronted with diverse sexual techniques and positions promising outerspace moments, many people are confused as to whether sexual activity is best enjoyed while being on top, below or hanging sideways from the ceiling. Extensive instruction manuals confirm that we lack sexual perfection and remind us of expectations to be fulfilled. Almost everywhere we turn, sex is used to entice us, to sell to us, to manipulate us or to otherwise capture our attention. Commonly, young women (many with implanted silicone floating devices) are displayed to create the notion that sex is only enjoyable with a perfect body. It is not surprising, that after watching *Striptease* with their man and glaring at Demi Moore's flawless body, women everywhere are reluctant to expose their bodies to their partners. Sadly, many women suffer in silence at the sight of their not-so-perfect bodies and have become quite industrious in inventing ways to hide them. Others spend lots of money, endure pain and use a great deal of time to achieve perfect bodies.

After discovering her husband's affair with her younger counterpart, Marla Maples, Ivana Trump spent a fortune and suffered considerable discomfort at the hands of one of the best plastic surgeons in the country. Amusingly, the new Ivana looked almost like Marla's identical twin, but Donald still refused to dump Marla. Ivana, on the other hand, had been completely overhauled just in time to sign her divorce papers, though I am sure her divorce settlement was sufficient to fund a number of subsequent surgeries. In mint condition, Ivana managed two more divorces in a hurry, while Donald replaced Marla many times over. It doesn't look like Donald underwent any plastic surgery to capture the most dazzling beauties, and maybe it is true that money and power have more sex appeal than an impeccable face and body.

Maintaining a flawless, youthful body and face is not as significant for men, as they are not depicted as sex objects to the same extent as women. Sex has become an over-rated subject and the cause of much unhappiness and frustration. How can we be comfortable with our own sexuality in a society that pressures us to have lots of sex that must be great every time?

Sex is by far a greater social issue for women as well as the root of much of their confusion and insecurity. Historically, women's primary sexual purpose was to be fertile and nurture the products of their fertility. As good wives, they were expected to provide sexual gratification whenever their husbands demanded it. Women didn't need to be aroused, let alone feel sexual desire or even have orgasms. In short, women were simply meant to bear children while men, living in a world of increased testosterone levels, demanded that women be available for sex.

With the advent of birth control, a sexual revolution began; and both men and women were able to enjoy sex without fear of pregnancy. Women experienced a tremendous sexual liberation. Since then, women's orgasmic abilities have been discovered and we are still debating heavily where and how their erogenous zones can best be targeted. Women have unleashed their sexual desires, their need for arousal and their potential for earth-shattering orgasms. An increasing number of women are demanding sexual fulfillment, an experience that for the longest time had been taken for granted by men.

Traditionally, men were viewed as hunters who conquered women; however, with the role reversal of the sexual revolution, many women are now hunting for their fair share of sexual gratification. Since Freud first described "penis envy," many women have discovered their own sexual capacity and no longer envy this powerful male instrument.

For many men, women's sexual liberation has caused performance pressure that consequently leads to performance anxiety. As a result, countless women fake orgasm hoping to make their partners feel good about a job well done. The magnitude and significance of sex in our society often produces a sexual relationship between lovers that resembles finely tuned high-performance race cars. It appears as though a mind-blowing orgasm is the final test of any sexual relationship. Entire industries are lining up with products to make it happen.

❤ A Sex-Saturated Population

Some examples of recent Internet advertisements claiming to help make your sex life outstanding:

INCREASE YOUR PENIS SIZE

Do you want a bigger penis?
Do you want to be hard as a rock all the time?
Do you want to pleasure your partner every time?

Proven medical techniques you can do RIGHT NOW which we've been studying and perfecting since 1994. These methods are effective, natural, and safe. You will learn guaranteed methods of increasing penis size that you can do right NOW in the privacy of your own home. Guaranteed results!! Thousands of men have tried our methods with great success! MONEY BACK GUARANTEE! NOTHING TO LOSE AND INCHES TO GAIN!

Do penises have to look like offshore drilling equipment to make it to the finishing line? It is no wonder that men with smaller penises feel that nature handed them a raw deal. Premature ejaculation and inability to maintain an erection seem to be main areas of discussion and research. For the most part the focus of research has been biased towards men's sexual improvement. Viagra®, for instance, increases the blood flow to the penis, causing it to remain erect for an extended period of time. Its arrival was a great success because it assisted men in their ability to perform. Viagra® even rekindled sexual interest in those men with only floppies to insert, men who withdrew from sex because of embarrassment and frustration. Erectile dysfunction may be caused by: penis abnormalities, circulatory problems, low testosterone, neural disorders, diabetes and substance abuse, as well as a number of other diseases, all of which are physiologically based and require professional treatment. However, erectile difficulties often have psychological causes, many of which can be directly linked to the type of relationships we have. This chapter will explore the psychologically related causes underlying erectile failure and lack of sexual desire, which reportedly are big areas of concern for both men and women.

❤ Sexual Dysfunction versus Dissatisfaction

For people of all ages the increased exposure to sex in our society has created much anxiety over being desirable and aroused enough to meet the requirements of acceptable sexual partners. Those of us who follow statistics on national averages of sexual frequency cannot help but compare how our own sex lives measure up. Still, we should keep in mind that these statistics are based on self-reports of participants. Frequencies of sexual activities fluctuate with levels of stress and are affected by our overall well-being. Most importantly, the frequency and extent of our sexual activities are directly linked to the level of intimacy in our relationships. Sexual desire and frequency often decline, as we get older. It has also been said that it may decline according to the length of a relationship. On the contrary, in many long-term, meaningful relationships, sexual frequency increases due to a heightened level of intimacy between partners. Less frequent sex as a result of biological changes appears to mostly affect people in their middle to older ages.

In conclusion, non-biological reasons for declining sexual activity, erectile failure and reduced sexual desire most often stem from unresolved relationship issues. When a relationship is characterized by sexual dissonance due to unresolved conflict, we often focus on the sexual disharmony and interpret this sexual discord as just one partner's fault.

Looking beyond the sexual problems of those in relationships who are physiologically healthy, there is always a lack of respect and *moral responsibility*. Consequently, the need for intimacy, trust and commitment remain unfulfilled. While it can be difficult for sexual desire to flourish with the pressures of daily chores, agendas and distraction, it is even more challenging when we are not deeply connected. Still we often label lack of sexual desire as a dysfunction needing treatment with libido-increasing remedies, both medical and non-medical.

According to recent statistics, *"desire on demand"* is selling "big time." Often, so-called sexual dysfunction is really sexual dissatisfaction arising from psychological causes such as lack of intimacy and communication. Are we confusing sexual dysfunction with sexual dissatisfaction, and precipitously popping pills to take sexual gratification to new heights? I believe many have come to rely on engineered sex-enhancing drugs, lotions and potions to create lust, desire and arousal, while ignoring intimacy in their sex lives.

A case in point is the example of women who failed to achieve orgasm in their present relationships, due to sexual dissatisfaction, but did reach orgasm when they engaged in an affair. I am not an advocate of women having affairs when they feel sexually frustrated; however, I would like to make the point that an inability to achieve orgasm is more often than not linked to a psychological cause involving lack of intimacy and respect.

Recent research indicates that an increasing number of

married women are having affairs, and they cite emotional neglect and sexual frustration as their reasons for doing so. This is obviously the result of the sexual liberation of women who have become aware of their own sexuality and ability to enjoy sexual intimacy. Many have become fairly discriminating and seek sexual pleasure for themselves. Over two-thirds of cheating women experienced orgasm in their affairs, even when they did not with their spouses. These results suggest that, at least in the above cases, the inability to achieve orgasm seems to be psychologically rather than clinically based. Maybe these cheating women believe themselves to be more intimate in their affairs than they do in their marriages. In summary, our minds have a lot more to do with the way we enjoy sex than we think, and, as you will see, the soul plays the biggest role in the creation of lasting love and meaningful sex lives.

I have heard many men complain about their partner's lack of interest in sex. These men often arrive at the conclusion that their female partners are simply not sexually inclined, do not enjoy sex and are either frigid or unresponsive. Truthfully, many women feel like physical objects designed for the pleasure of their partner while their own satisfaction is neglected. Consequently women often feel that they are just having sex instead of making love. Simply stated, there are very few women who do not like making love and far more who are drawn to the idea of loving their partners through sexual intimacy. However, many women just don't like the way they have sex or are made love to, and they are afraid of telling their partners how they feel.

Even though dissatisfying sex lives appear to be a main reason for affairs among couples, the underlying cause is mostly friction and conflict in other areas of the relationship. I have encountered straying lovers who actually claimed that an affair had revived their relationship, such as in the case of Darby and

Roger. Darby was frustrated that Roger did not take time to arouse her prior to intercourse and was even more upset by his premature ejaculation. Their sex life seemed for his benefit only, and she was convinced that Roger's inconsiderate five-minute sex routine was the reason for their marital problems. When she met Mel at the office, she felt perfectly within her rights to seek what she was missing in her marriage. Darby's affair with Mel lasted over a year and while she felt sexually fulfilled, balancing both relationships became increasingly difficulty. Mel ended their affair when Roger discovered his wife's infidelity. Roger, unaware of Darby's sexual frustration, never suspected (or so he said) that she was capable of betraying him. Ironically, Darby and Roger both reported an improved sex life after the detection of her affair. Now their sexual interludes extended from five minutes to ten and became an act of two emotionally beaten people instead of lovemaking. Roger's pride had been attacked and his ego wounded, but he decided to forgive Darby, who did not care about the consequences of her affair. Instead, she felt deserted by Mel who ended the affair against her wishes. It did not take long for Darby to seek another affair, only this time she was more careful about not getting caught. Roger and Darby still live their lives with lies and deception and are only tied together through habit and fear of change. Both avoid the real issue in their relationship, which is the lack of emotional connectedness and, as a result, they do not know each other at all. More importantly they are not yet *fit to love* each other.

True emotional connectedness is only possible in the presence of *mutual respect* and *moral responsibility*. As I stated before, when you respect another and feel morally responsible, you do not lie, cheat or belittle your partner in any way. Instead you have a desire to know this person right down to the core. You respect his or her needs, views and beliefs as you do your own and, most importantly, you do not act morally irresponsibly. Being unfaithful is disrespectful, morally irresponsible and never a solution to the problems in a relationship. As a matter of fact, it is the ultimate form of betrayal, the devastating consequences of which can almost never be erased.

You may disagree with me and point to relationships that have continued after an affair. You may also think of relationships that exist under mutual permission to engage in sexual encounters outside of the relationship. People can forgive, pretend to forget and even rationalize an affair, but they can never make them go away. Seemingly forgiven and forgotten affairs will always be the one cracked brick that makes the house crumble, even if all the other bricks have weathered the storm. Like a weak link, overcome affairs will snap the chain when someone rattles it.

Many relationship experts argue that relationships can be mended and even improved after an affair. While this might be true, I believe that the pain, distrust and degradation caused by an affair can never be completely erased and, in some ways, it is like the scars of childhood abuse. The abused can learn to think differently about it, learn to live with it, make the best out of it, cope with it, but can never make it go away. Often, when a couple stays together after an affair, it is for reasons that have very little to do with love, and sooner or later they split up anyway. Still, it is a personal choice whether to forgive an affair and stay together or to end the relationship.

If a relationship is to survive an affair (as few do) the purest and surest way to starting over is through sexual abstinence. Respect, responsibility and love cannot be established in bed. Leaving sex out of the equation for a few months allows you to see who the other person really is and relate more honestly to each other. Sexual abstinence empowers partners, re-builds self-respect and helps you realize that sex is not just about gratification, rather it is the ultimate gift to give to each other.

As responsible adults we can completely avoid exposing our mates to the traumatizing effects of infidelity. Yet in over 40 percent of relationships, at least one partner believes it to be his or her right to have an affair at the cost of their partner's pain. Such was the case with Darby, whose affair continued to be a cover-up for underlying issues in her relationship. She didn't feel loved and respected by Roger, nor did she feel emotionally connected to him. Understandably she became frustrated, since emotional connectedness is vital for the growth of any intimate relationship.

There can be no doubt that the meaningfulness and enjoyment of lovemaking in a relationship is directly related to the degree of emotional intimacy. Without emotional intimacy, we experience sex simply as a vehicle towards the "Big O." For Roger, just having sex with Darby was enough and he did not require anything more meaningful. As a matter of fact, he could not understand why making love is such a big deal. But if we are to experience true love in and out of bed, making love is a *BIG* deal and an act of the soul. Unless Roger and Darby are willing to deal with the issues of respect and *moral responsibility*, their relationship will never become meaningful or ever develop into real love. For now, Roger feels challenged to overcome the hurt of Darby's affair, whereas she only feels validated when she is engaged in an affair.

Rationalization of affairs is fairly common. As John, a soon-to-be-married man, said: "It wasn't until after I cheated on my girlfriend, that I knew she was the right one. If I hadn't done that, I would have never been sure. Being unfaithful helped me become committed to my girlfriend." Who are you trying to fool, John?

Even though Hollywood attempts to romanticize and glamorize affairs, in real life they are little more than a means to satisfy sexual and/or emotional desires. Infidelity definitely lacks the elements of *mutual respect* and *moral responsibility*. With rare exception, those with whom you have affairs are not those to whom you want to commit. The classic example of affairs between single women and married men demonstrates my point very well. When a single woman becomes involved with a married man, she does so *knowing* that he is not available for a relationship of *mutual respect* and *moral responsibility*.

After her 10-year affair with Ernie, Averil, a beautiful and bright young woman, found herself emotionally depleted with little self-esteem. To keep their affair a secret, Averil had to agree to his terms regarding time spent together and places to go. Ernie gave her an account of his miserable wife, who had no interest in sex. In her attempt to rate favorably against Ernie's wife, Averil remained compliant and demand-free. She used her most thrilling seduction techniques in the hope that someday she would win him over. Someday never came and she began to make demands on him to leave his wife. As a conflict avoider, Ernie was unable to decide between the two women in his life. Averil survived on his promise to leave his wife, and the fact that he was even considering a divorce made her feel quite special. When Ernie finally left his wife, Averil saw the real Ernie instead of her romanticized version of him. All of sudden, Ernie was no longer as attractive, charming, generous and complimentary as she had thought. After 10 years of being with someone who could not commit, Averil had lost much of her self-respect, dignity and pride, and finally realized that Ernie was not able to commit to his wife or to her.

Affairs are mostly recreational power plays in which we think ourselves powerful enough to conquer one person at the emotional and financial expense of another. In the triangle of an affair, all parties are victims, and the betrayed, often-unsuspecting partner, is usually blamed as soon as he or she learns of the infidelity. This must be one of the most reckless and irresponsible forms of behavior towards another human being. The disastrous consequences affect not only those directly involved, but extend to family members and friends. Children of the fractured pair are the most innocent victims even if they are unaware of the betrayal. They are exposed to an unhealthy relationship that will become the blueprint for their own future. We have no right to expose our children to the demoralizing effects of our self-gratification. We do, however, have an obligation to make our relationships the best they can be, and setting this example is one of the most loving, meaningful and lasting gifts we can give to our children.

❤ We Are All Natural Experts at Sex

We are sexual beings and unless we suffer from a clinical dysfunction, we are natural experts at sex. Our bodies do know how to love through sexual closeness, if only we allow our souls to open up. When we truly love another person our soul overflows and becomes the loving force of sexual intimacy. If our soul embraces another without hesitation we are making love and there are no barriers to sexual fulfillment. Making love is the most profound, intimate and meaningful connection with another human being. If we allow sexual interaction to become a static fixture instead of an abundant source of love, we are cheating ourselves (and our partners) of the most powerful way to unearth the deepest emotions in each other.

Too often, the success of our relationships is measured by the greatness of our sex lives. Sex seems to be a powerful drug that impairs our judgment in many areas, in particular, at the onset of a new relationship. By over-emphasizing sex, we often develop relationships under faulty judgment and neglect aspects that later crystallize into more severe problems.

For example, when I asked Timothy about his new girlfriend, Dana, an interesting dialog developed:

"How is your new romance progressing?"
"The sex is great and we have lots of fun."
"What is Dana like?"
"She is very attractive and sexy. She is a web designer and works downtown."
"Anything else about her?"
"I am crazy about her."

Immersed in sex, Timothy was too clouded to really get to know Dana and it was not until well into their relationship that he discovered many incompatibilities. One of them was Dana's need for a continuous supply of new sexual partners in order to be excited. Timothy's heart was broken, his confidence shattered, and he had contracted a sexually transmitted disease.

Relationships consist of five components: social (background, education and social class), sexual (physical attraction and chemistry), spiritual (mental and or religious orientation), ethical (values, beliefs and morals) and goals (occupation, interests and activities). While their importance may vary at any given time, each of these five components should be of more or less equal priority. For instance, a change in career may take priority over the other components at the time when the career change takes place. Unfortunately, we often fail to maintain the 20 percent balance of each of these components and allow sex to inhabit more than its 20 percent share. As a result, many evaluate their relationship on the basis of the perceived quality or quantity of sexual activities. When there is lots of sex and the sex is good, then the relationship must be good, and vice versa. In point of fact, a relationship can be terrible in spite of lots of good sex.

Many singles believe that there is nothing wrong with sex on the first date or in the early stages of a new relationship. After all, they need to find out if the person is good in bed and if they are sexually compatible. Exploring the sexual capabilities of a new partner is obviously much easier than introducing him or her to one's parents. I have always wondered why so many people sleep with people whom they are not prepared to introduce to their families. TV shows such as *Blind Date* (I must watch these programs to be a well-informed relationship coach) portray first dates that frequently include undressing and jumping into the hot tub. I have to ask myself if these speed-dating methods requiring full body exposure aren't putting the horse before the cart, or if I missed some important cues during my own encounters.

We are natural experts at sex simply because a relatively healthy body is designed to express love through its own perfect sexuality. Sadly, many people pay too much attention to the widespread societal beliefs about sex. Often we believe that having a better body would improve our sex lives or that pornography would ad zest. Many refer to the "how-to" sex manual in an attempt to get it right. How can we be comfortable with our own sexuality when we adopt someone else's beliefs about sex? Too often when we have sex we are so overly concerned with how we look, breathe, smell, sound and move that we fail to trust our own bodies. Wrapped up in the details and technicalities of sexual performance, we do not allow ourselves to engage in the natural flow of our well-orchestrated bodies. For many, the "Big O" is the significant outcome of sexual interaction and sexual encounters are guided with this goal in mind. The orgasm becomes the main focus, the topic of discussion, the scale of success, the reason to have sexual contact and, ultimately, the final test of the relationship.

Despite the suggestion of *Cosmopolitan*, our bodies do not require instruction manuals or enhanced techniques in the quest for even greater sexual satisfaction or higher voltage orgasms. Is it really necessary to generate enough orgasmic voltage to light up an entire airport, particularly if you consider its duration, however intense?

The body operates in synergy with the mind. If we separate mind from body, only our bodily desires guide us through the sexual act. We become performance oriented, focus on our own level of excitement, and rate our partner based on how exciting or thrilling he or she is. We cheat our hearts by excluding our souls, and we abandon the deepest and innermost connection with another human being. While sex can be a relieving experience for the body, sex in itself is never love. Sex maybe the icing on the cake, but making love is the cake with icing and so much more than sex alone could ever be.

What makes our bodies healthy and normal so we can have the confidence of being natural experts at making love? How can we feel proud of our bodies even when they do not measure up to an ideal? Let's go back to the mind and body connection and explore how our mind perceives our body and determines our image.

I would like to use the example of 30-year-old Marsha, who shopped in stores for clothes where even an anorexic person would be hard pressed to close a zipper. She perceived herself to be overweight and gaining. To add to her grief, she found numerous flaws in herself, such as being too short (you don't have to be tall to reach for the stars), too small busted, too small eyed, too narrow lipped, too long nosed and her list of too this or too that went on forever. By the time she was through with her self-critique, she was convinced nobody could possibly be interested in her, let alone love her. The end of her last relationship had been highly predictable. Her negative self-image did not allow her to love without hesitation and any lovemaking attempt ended in disaster. Objectively, Marsha was five-foot-three, not too skinny or too heavy, had a pretty face, well-defined nose, and healthy hair. In truth, like most people in this world, she was of average attractiveness. She even had a wonderful smile in those few moments when she was happy. Unfortunately, her mind was focused on the perceived imperfections of her body, instead of feeling all there is to feel when making love.

For the most part, the image we have of our body is more negative than it is positive, yet it is almost never objective. No matter how negative it may be, our body image guides much of what we do or don't do. We often believe that with an imperfect body we are being excluded from certain enjoyments, and this affects our confidence level adversely. Often the way we see our own body is simply a perception of our minds. If we would stop comparing ourselves to the ideals of society, we would recognize that most bodies are simply normal and average.

The healthy, well-tuned body is a body that is honored and respected. What does it mean to honor one's body? It means being aware that you were given one body only, intended to last a lifetime. While you can fix many of its broken parts, this amazingly engineered machine must take you through all the days of your life. When you honor your body you treat it with kindness, nurture it, pamper it, fuel it well, take pride in it, move it and use it, regardless of whether you believe it to be perfect. You maintain the strength of your body and the power of your brain. Whenever you let your body or mind slip backwards, your life will slip with it. Your body and brain are designed to be active.

When you challenge both, your life will turn around. How your body looks is secondary to how you feel in your body. When you put your body in motion and your brain into gear, you feel upbeat and hopeful about life and are in tune with yourself. Moreover, if you take pride in your body and challenge your brain, you are physically and mentally alive and strong. You will then experience the power to feel and sense everything from within. Every body deserves to be honored, cherished, pampered and respected, regardless of its shape.

To develop a strong body through motion you can run, walk, bicycle or swim, engage in sports, roller-blade, hike, dance or do whatever activity you enjoy. While it is not necessary to belong to a fitness club, I must admit that being a long-time member of a health club has given me a sense of mastery and discipline over my body. As I worked my imperfect body, among other mostly imperfect bodies, it became stronger and so did my senses. I became aware of my body, began to enjoy it and everything it can do, in particular, making love. My body is still far from perfect, however, being in tune with the power and capabilities of my body has changed the way I perceive myself. Instead of going through life in a physical structure that I detested, I now walk with pride and no longer expect perfection from my body. Even though this is not a health or fitness book, you need to make the connection between body and mind and understand how it relates to being a natural expert at making love. Being "in sync" with your body and in touch with your soul is the foundation of both a meaningful love relationship and satisfying sex life. Accepting your body for its strengths and uniqueness is much more powerful than admiring your body for its attractiveness.

Each part of your body is designed for movement and the entire energy flow of your body depends how it is being fueled.

In other words, your body will put out what you put into it and therefore the choice of nutrients is important. While I do not want to get carried away here, I believe it is vital to shed some light on the confusion about nutrition. The array of diets on the market range from cabbage diets, high protein, low carbohydrates, fat free to the next-to-nothing diet. The bottom line is you need a bit of everything and you need it every day in a balanced way. It is true that your body does not need chocolate, booze, chips, French fries, ice cream and other nutritionally deficient foods, but your soul might need these useless foods from time to time. When investigating diets, pay attention to their sensibility and whether your body receives all the important nutrients on a daily basis.

Throughout my years of trying to maintain my weight and consuming a sensible balance of nutrients, I have probably come across just as many diets as you have. Among all these diets you will find a few which are levelheaded and have stood the test of time. One of them, *Food-Combining*, has proven itself for over 20 years. *Food-Combining* is simply a way of eating unprocessed foods in accordance with your body's requirements while separating carbohydrates from proteins during each meal. This is just one of a few examples of eating sensibly, that is simple and easy to follow.

The way we enjoy life and love has a lot more to do with how we feel about ourselves than with how attractive we are. I do not believe for even a moment that these "knockout" bodies popping up on the screen or in magazines have more success in finding lasting love than you or I do. Nor do I believe that their lovemaking is more rewarding or meaningful than yours or mine. Honor your body, fuel it, move it, cherish it and know that every part of it is a gift of life. Your body may be just one of many bodies in the world, but you are and can be one special person to someone.

❤ Making Love: *Revealing the fragile self*

What is the difference between sex and making love? This million-dollar question generated a million answers among those asked, and I could have filled this book with an abundance of valid and interesting answers. However, I will get to the point because no matter how many answers I read, making love is about revealing your Fragile Self.

First of all, when one claims to have made love on the first date, you and I know that this is not possible. At the very best you can lust after someone but you can't make love with someone whom you do not yet love. On the first date or even early in a relationship we appraise the other person based on their appearance. While he or she may be a delight or a source of physical pleasure, it is definitely not love. Making love is a total mind and body event and when you make love you listen with your heart and hear the other person's soul.

> *Having sex is about you, making love is about us.*
> —Author Unknown

While having sex is about bodily satisfaction, making love involves nurturing the soul. Most of us doubt our ability to love unconditionally and resent the idea of becoming vulnerable. We believe vulnerability renders us powerless, grants another control over us and allows us to get hurt. However, our real power lies in accepting our fragile human egos and fearlessly facing our vulnerability as humble beings. In hiding our true self, we remain severed from each other's energy and never give ourselves wholly to another person.

Completely opening your heart to the one you love and showing your fragile soul is the reality of love. When you no longer doubt your own ability to love, you feel safe to expose your soul in total nakedness and you can finally make love; until then you will only have sex. Anyone can share his or her body with anybody at any given time. Making love is surrendering fully to one another and becoming part of something larger than oneself. It is about knowing that your body and soul are worthy of being shared with the one person you love and no one else.

More than anything, making love is about knowing what you really mean to one another. It is about exposing your heart, your feelings and re-establishing a soulful commitment. *When someone really knows you the way you know yourself, and still loves you, you can finally make love.* When you have sex your body may be satisfied but your soul continues to hunger. You may have hit the jackpot with your joystick, but your heart has not cashed in. Making love breaks the facades you have built around yourself and stirs emotions you never thought you had. When you have sex there is no lasting meaning attached to it. When you make love you build emotional history with another being. This is why making love is one of the most powerful human moments on earth. The power of love can be expressed through lovemaking much more strongly than through words.

Among all the relationships in your life, there is only one in which you share the soulful act of making love. You do not make love to your relatives, children or friends and, in that sense, your intimate relationship with this one person becomes sacred. This is the powerful difference between those you love and the one precious person with whom you share your life, body and soul. In making love you can show how much you care for this person. Through gentleness and respect you realize your own power to love. By stretching your heart as you make love, you love all the wounds, pains and struggles of the other and you can make him or her feel exceptional.

On a physical level, when you make love you do not focus on the imperfections of yourself or partner, nor do you get caught up in the technicalities of doing it right. Instead, you are deeply aware that, through the innermost connection and emotional intensity, you are making love with someone who trusts you with body and soul. Making love is about being intimate without thinking of orgasm as the final goal. While orgasm may or may not happen, the unhurried human moments before and after orgasm are what define lovemaking. Sexual behavior and experiences may change over the course of a relationship, but the growing depth in which you and your lover connect through lovemaking does not. There is nothing more exciting and exhilarating than sharing body and soul with each other. Experiencing true lovemaking depends on whether you believe in your own ability to love.

What exactly are those human moments before and after orgasm? The answers from the many men and women I asked had nothing to do with orgasm:

"When I hold and kiss her body all over, including her stretch-marks and cellulite thighs, my body and soul feel restored. It is then that I know that through the strength of our love we can overcome anything."

"When he looks at me in total nakedness and whispers loving and caring words into my ears, I feel the excitement over growing old with him."

"When I kiss her passionately while our eyes lock, I get in touch with the meaning of 'I love you' and know I never want to be without her."

"When we make love it is about total honesty, emotional risk and the orgasm is just the final moment."

"When I watch her fall asleep after we made love I feel overwhelmed by my emotions and just want to wrap myself around her and keep her safe."

*If you live to be a hundred, I want to live to be a
hundred minus one day,
so I never have to live without you.*
—Winnie the Pooh

Many people define their relationships by standards other than just sex. Those who are deeply in love also have active and enriching sex lives. Their lovemaking nurtures their souls and deepens their commitment as they embrace and cherish each other's bodies and souls. As I stated before, making love is the most fulfilling way to express your profound feelings for another person. In letting this experience take hold of you, you are taking your heart and body to a better place. Maybe making the choice to be emotionally vulnerable and to love with all that you are is the simple secret to meaningful sexual intimacy.

Sadly, there are many relationships in which making love has been put on the back burner. Sex is either scarce or absent, and when it does occur, it is often difficult. Numerous healthy couples with sexually functioning bodies treat their sex lives like collector's items that occasionally receive a good dusting, only to be put back on the shelf again. While most people in these cooled relationships would secretly like to play around with their collector's piece more often, the topic of sex is no longer up for discussion as it creates more resentment than any other issue. Like running water wears away a rock, this resentment wears away the bridge to intimacy, but partners still need to cross the water and talk about it.

For otherwise healthy couples a diminishing sex life is a good indicator of serious trouble in their relationship. No one should ever underestimate the power and importance of making love. Lovemaking is a main contributor to intimacy and creates warm thoughts of our partners. It is rather difficult to blow up at your mate after you had a wonderful experience. It is absolutely normal and even desirable to want to make love to our partner as often as possible and when we do not, we need to find out why. Instead of assuming (remember the discussion about assuming in chapter 8) why the other has little or no interest in lovemaking, and instead of blaming one another, we must seek the truth.

The main reasons for the decline in lovemaking or its absence among healthy couples are emotional disconnectedness and build-up of resentment. I know you are able to list a million other reasons such as stress (sex actually counteracts stress), lack of time (it is amazing how even the busiest person can find time for what he or she deems important), headaches (by the way sex is a great headache relief), being tired (often a mindset when we do not like the way we have sex), feeling unattractive (great sex does not require a great body), or simply not liking sex. Those reasons are simply sub-categories of the two above main reasons.

Couples who are emotionally close and maintain active and meaningful sex lives are also tired, cope with stress, do not have enough time, suffer from headaches, are not necessarily attractive and even have children. Even though the presence of children often discourages couples from making love, it is not necessary to retreat to a hotel every time they feel the "urge to merge." Seeing their parents in love and knowing they make love creates a tremendous amount of security and faith for children.

Couples who enjoy sex with each other have made their relationship, and therefore love, a priority in their lives. When love takes precedence, our heart is primed and our body follows. Even in light of varying sexual appetites, making love becomes a matter of accommodating each other rather than a power struggle. When couples have shown their vulnerable selves to each other they are able to express their sexual desires and preferences without blame and accusation. If lovemaking seriously declines or ceases to exist, it is time to talk and find out why the two of you no longer do what you used to enjoy. When both talk openly and fairly about sex there is nothing to lose and everything to gain (love, in its most intimate way). Most people find it difficult to talk about sex and, unfortunately, discussions often start with accusations, such as, "You are always this or that," or "You never do one thing or another."

I have heard many excuses from, "She always wants sex" to "He is never interested," or vice versa. Generally people do not always want sex or never want sex. Our sex lives are not a one-man or one-woman show and both parties are responsible for the outcome. It is not even a 50/50 affair; like anything in your relationship it requires 100% from each person. We must negotiate our sexual desires, expectations, dreams and hopes with mutual respect and moral responsibility, in simple terms, with the good will of a loving heart.

Those who have lost that "loving feeling" need to start over and rebuild their relationships on a stronger foundation. How dare we not ask each other how to make our relationships the best they can be!

How do we prevent boredom in the bedroom? How can we keep romance alive? Do we have to show up in mink coats with nothing underneath, or light 50 candles to get the juices flowing? While you might want to consult publications providing a plethora of advice on these questions, I will tell you this: One of the biggest turn-ons is initiating lovemaking with your partner because it makes him or her feel wanted, needed, desired and above all loved. You can do any, all or none of the above and by all means be adventurous. You can employ any other bright idea or technique you come across, and many do so successfully.

In ending this chapter I would like to address the subject of "men and sex." I have chosen to do so because of two common beliefs that still linger with us. The first belief is that women are more interested in the romantic aspects of lovemaking and this has already been addressed in this book. The second belief is that men largely aim for the Big O and are inconsiderate both before and after this main event. I feel inclined to defend many of the men I interviewed on this subject.

The majority of men will notice an attractive woman; however, for those men who do think with their main brain (luckily they are in the majority), the biggest turn-on is the challenging and caring mind of a woman. Those seeking a loving relationship of respect and responsibility do care very much about the core of the woman they date or eventually marry.

It may come as a surprise to you, but most men do think of other things apart from sex. They believe in lasting friendship, romance, true love, they have goals and dreams and, of course, they want sex. Why wouldn't men want to make love to their wives or girlfriends knowing how wonderful it is?

The good news is that men, in particular those under the age of 50, have become much more sensitive and receptive towards relationships of equality. The best news I have for women out there is that these men do enjoy the giving and receiving in equitable unions and would like to see their relationships work for both. Surprisingly, for many men the Big O is not necessarily the most glorified moment of lovemaking and they are just as moved by the moments before and after.

When men are truly in love, here is what they know and cherish about their mate:

- They do know the difference between sex and making love.
- They love to give pleasure.
- They enjoy looking into her eyes when making love.
- They love it when she initiates lovemaking.
- If they respect her, they love her whole body including all its flaws.
- They like permission to be weak and vulnerable without being judged.
- They love to cuddle and feel safe.
- They love to watch her fall asleep and wake up.
- They like both "quickies" and extended lovemaking.
- When intimate, they like to sometimes be serious, and funny at other times.
- Above all they want to be loved for all that they are, just like she does.
- They want to make love because it feels good.

To put it simply, as long as your body permits you to make love, use your body and rejoice in sexual intimacy with the one you love.

❤ 5 Principles to Remember from Chapter Nine

1. Through the soulful act of making love you build an emotional history with the other person.
2. When you no longer doubt your own ability to love, you can finally make love.
3. Your well-equipped body knows how to express the power of love through its own perfect sexuality.
4. Having sex is about you, making love is about both of you.
5. Honoring your body for its strength and uniqueness is more powerful than admiring your body for its attractiveness.

CHAPTER 10

"WHAT IS THIS THING CALLED LOVE?"
Love Is a Choice: Choose It or Lose It.

When my mom looks at my dad's beer-belly and asks if he has lost weight.
—SARAH, 10

When my dad cleans the house and gives all the loose change to mom.
—BRIAN, 5

When my grandma brushes my grandpa's teeth and then puts them in a glass.
—ALLISON, 6

LOVE IS . . . ! A multitude of meanings could fill in the blanks. We all need to fill in the blanks and make sense of the meaning of love. While we may each have our own unique definition, it would be much simpler if someone, somewhere, sometime soon, offered a universal definition of love. With an international, all-inclusive definition, we would all know what love really is and, more importantly, we would finally know whether it exist in our lives. But even with a universal definition, we would most likely argue over its interpretation and, in the end, we would be no further ahead. What, then, is this thing called "Love?"

Not merely does love have very diverse meanings to each of us, these meanings change throughout our lives. Love means something entirely different at the age of 20 than it does at a more mature age. Moreover, the ways in which we love alter drastically over the course of our lives. Just as the meaning of love changes through our experiences, so do the forces of love change us as we mature. The absence or presence of love in your life ultimately determines who you become. Love is the lifeblood of our psychological make-up and for those who did not receive love, there is much catching up to do.

Unless love is unconditional, it will always be subject to interpretation and is never a straightforward concept. Love can be a dual edged sword, cutting deeply, or a multifaceted crystal of sanity. Love in itself is full of contradictions and we would be challenged to define a loving person. Love entails so many opposites because we ourselves are complex and filled with contradictions. That alone makes love one of the most complex and highly debated issues on this planet. However, we all have one thing in common: we need love. All of us desire unconditional love because there is an immense validation in knowing that we are being loved, "no matter what."

Many refer to unconditional love as *being loved for who you are*. I would like to clarify this cliché. In truth, you cannot be loved for who you are, simply because you are always changing even though your values may not. You can never again be who you were yesterday and you cannot be today who you are about to become tomorrow. Being loved for who you are simply means being loved just because you exist. There is nothing you have to do or say to earn this love. Is that kind of love possible? You better believe it. However, most of us have to confront all of love's contradictions before we can embrace unconditional love. Unless you are willing to love more today than you did yesterday, you will remain a victim of love's contradictions. When someone says, "No one will ever love you the way I do," that person is speaking the truth. We never love the same way twice. Each time we love, we either love less, more or altogether differently. The reason why we should love more each time will become apparent to you while reading this chapter. Love is the journey through life, and unconditional love is life's final destination. Some of us arrive there while others do not. The difference lies in the choices we make along the way, and which meaning we choose to attach to love.

Love has so many paradoxes and opposing interpretations. Love can alter even the most hopeless of circumstances and transform lives. Love can change all of our intentions, every goal and every rule. Love defeats time, erases adversity and turns dreams into reality. Love presents us with a conundrum and at the same time it releases us from doubt. For some, love is like a rescue and for others it is a danger. Love gives us the strength to rise above as it breaks down the walls around us. Love speaks to us when we are silent and touches us in invisible ways when we least expect it. Love can cause pain and yet heal our most aching wounds. In love we lose and in love we gain. Those who love us are our heroes, while those who stop loving us become our enemies. Love may cause defeat, but it also lets us triumph by leading us out of the shadow into the light. No matter how mysterious love may be to each of us, all our hearts feel the same pains and joys of love, even though our lives and beliefs may be quite different.

> *Never forget that the most powerful force*
> *on earth is love.*
> —NELSON ROCKEFELLER

Falling in love and being in love is like being overcome by a landslide of wonderful mental and bodily energies, and that may be one of the reasons we want to be in love. However, if loving means "I love you, but—," you love with limits and conditions. In this sense your love is crippled and supported by a crutch.

Love is a choice and you can choose between two kinds of love: conditional or unconditional. Which kind of love you unleash depends on the type of love you are able or willing to give. In choosing conditional love, you place conditions upon that love and, in return, you must accept the conditions imposed by the other person. If you choose to love conditionally you will likely have to accept being loved under certain conditions. As long as the conditions are being mutually satisfied, the relationship will continue. In the event that the conditions can no longer be fulfilled and renegotiating proves unsuccessful, the relationship will become dissatisfying or even end. Conditional love is much like a game of cards and often you find yourself with "no aces to play."

Should you choose unconditional love, you are choosing love with staying power. With unconditional love your heart always knows its place, you always know where you are going and what you will do next. In other words, you will always have purpose and instead of simply living you will have something to live for. Unconditional love demands nothing and gives everything. Having the courage to love unconditionally means always believing and overcoming the obstacles by going the extra mile. Nothing you or I do in our lives will ever matter as much as the way we love.

> *For one human being to love another, that is perhaps the most difficult of our tasks, the ultimate, the last test and proof, the work for which all other work is but preparation.*
> —Rainer Maria Rilke

We all need a place for our hearts and want to feel safe when we set our hearts free. No matter how independent or self-sufficient we are, we still need each other to form the circle of life around us. Anything we do is unimportant if we do it only for ourselves. Anything we feel means very little if it cannot be shared. No matter how strong or resilient we think we are, strength and resilience are temporary attributes of a person. Even the toughest stumble and fall, regardless of how confident and self-trusting we may be. Our confidence becomes crushed and our self-trust shaken. Often we are unable to stand tall on our own. We are challenged to restore our faith and feel we are losing ground.

The idea of being complete on our own and not needing one another is an illusion created through the emergence of independence. In truth, we have always needed and will always need each other. Above all, each one of us needs to know that someone will be there until the end, regardless of whether we have risen to the top or fallen flat on our face. In our search for that someone we encounter unapproachable people, silent voices and empty faces, because most of us are hiding behind the illusion of independence. In reality, we are all interdependently connected in the web of life. Interdependence is a mature concept that recognizes even the most self-contained and competent person can accomplish very little in solitude.

If you are interdependent you realize your need for giving and receiving love even when your sense of self-worth is strong. Interdependence is the awareness that you need one another and knowing that you need to be needed as well. Contrary to the glorified concept of independence, being needed makes us feel precious. When we are not needed, we feel inadequate.

As young children we need our parents, even though we become more self-sufficient as we grow. The fact that we need someone who needs us does not stop when we reach a certain age. A part of this fragile, vulnerable child remains within us, makes us need someone and yearns to be needed no matter how much we deny it. We want to belong, and the most humble way of telling others what they mean to us is by letting them know that they are needed. Intimate relationships in which partners truly need each other are by far more successful because both feel valuable and irreplaceable.

Like many, you may ask why someone would need you. Do not waste another thought on this question. It is up to the other person to figure out why you are needed in his or her life. Just know that you are special and unique. In all of time there has never been anyone like you, and through all of eternity there will never be anyone with your given set of qualities. No other person thinks like you and no one will ever look like you. No one will ever laugh like you or shed tears the way you do. Above all, maybe God made you unique so you can do a special job that no one else can do in the same way.

Even though we all seek and need love in our lives, not everyone is willing to develop the mindset to feel and give unconditional love. Far too many lack the courage to believe in love and are not prepared to develop the human conduct and selflessness to make true love happen. Many seem to have lots of data and so-called facts about love, yet they remain clueless. I have already explained that human nature is bi-polar in the sense that whenever we are capable of feeling hate, anger or apathy, we can also feel the opposite, love. Likewise, if we have no faith in love we are still capable of finding it.

Love is a choice and when you choose it wholeheartedly you are never going to lose it. There will no longer be room in your heart for negative, soul-eroding feelings. Love teaches you who you are, challenges you to become a better human being, and gives you a sneak preview of who you ought to become. Maybe that is why so many fear love, for it asks you to take a serious look at your human conduct and change it. If you do not stand up for love, you don't stand for much of anything. Only through loving can you can make an eternal contribution to someone's life or humankind.

You must keep your faith in love at any cost, because if you lose this vision your heart expires. If you choose love, you choose a direct path to prosperity in all areas of your life. Maybe love will simply choose you and when it does, there is no escaping. You may not be able to keep this love but you will never forget the power of it.

> *Neither a lofty degree of intelligence nor imagination nor both together go to the making of a genius. Love, love, love, that is the soul of a genius.*
> —SAMUEL ADAMS, AMERICAN REVOLUTIONARY (1722–1893)

Why does love begin, grind to a standstill or completely end? Looking back over past relationships, often their beginnings and endings remain a mystery, even when you think you have figured it out. There are still unanswered questions: How can someone who claimed to love you (or so you thought) fall out of love and vice versa? In anticipation of future relationships (and I hope and pray that you will find the real thing), you may wonder if your next relationship will be yet another mystery. Apart from the obvious reason why lovers leave or stay, relationships are a mystery because of our own poor choices. We often stay in a relationship when we should leave, and leave when we should stay. While you can resolve the question of whether to stay or leave in many ways, let me explain how to handle this problem with dignity.

When neither of you is *fit to love* nor able to build unconditional love, you may still stay together (not much to be gained) or part company (not much to be lost). If you are *fit to love*, but the other is not, you must realize that love may not rest in the other person's spirit. All you can do then is touch with your loving spirit, but you cannot force love onto someone. You can either choose to live in emotional distance with one another and forego being loved wholly (a disempowering compromise), or let go and give your love to someone who wants it. If someone really loves you but you are unable to return this love, be honored, but do not use the person. Instead, refuse to take the loving gift that you cannot return and keep your soul clean.

> *Love teaches you how to fly, but you cannot soar like an eagle around chickens.*
> —Author Unknown

❤ Unconditional Love

What is the true measure of love?

> *When we believe that we alone can love in that way, that no one could ever have loved so before us and that no one will ever love in the same way after us.*
> —Johann Wolfgang Goethe

I asked my friend who has been happily married for 27 years, which were the best years of his marriage. He answered, "The first 27 years." While this is an impressive and touching statement, the real question is, how did he come to feel this way? For starters, when he said, "I do," he meant it. When problems arose he said, "I will do it better," and he did. When he said, "I love you," he meant: "I love you no matter what." When his love was challenged, he made the choice to love even more. Remember that in loving your heart knows no limits. Only you set limits. This couple made the choice to love with all that it entails, and they chose to respect, honor and to be morally responsible to one another. In so doing, they resolved conflict in goodwill and met each other's needs as best as possible. Knowing they both did their utmost, they never resented each other for needs gone unfulfilled.

When two people make the choice to love "no matter what," they open up their authentic self to each other. Knowing the body, mind and soul of another as you know yourself creates the emotional closeness that also fuels the desire for sexual intimacy. Quitting is never an option. This love is rock-solid and unbreakable. Even when life circumstances change, their love remains stable, dependable and most importantly, consistent. Couples who love this way have acquired the human conduct to be *fit to love* and may have received a little help from "Above."

To be *fit to love*, human conduct requires *mutual respect* and *moral responsibility*.

Mutual Respect: You are never more important than your partner and you honor his or her dreams, hopes, views, feelings and beliefs as you honor yours, for this person is just as valuable as you are. You support and help each other in being happy. If both cannot agree on a solution to solve a conflict, you realize that you will not always agree. Instead of arguing to be right, you agree to disagree and maintain a dialogue. Instead of resenting the other for not being what you expect, you both are committed to figuring out how to be better for each other. This is a tall order requiring humility and selflessness. On the other side of the coin, you can lose respect for the other when his or her conduct undermines your integrity and forces you to live at variance with your authentic self. There is no true love without respect and selflessness.

Moral Responsibility: Everything you think and do directly or indirectly affects those around you. You must consider the impact of your thoughts and actions on your mate. Even though you are responsible for your own happiness, when you truly love, you are responsible for your partner's well-being. You simply cannot gamble your life savings away or go on vacation with the girls, when your husband needs you. You must think of your partner as being just as important as you are and sometimes you will have to think of him or her first. Again, another tall order that requires selflessness. It is here where I like to pose the *wheelchair question:* Will you still love your partner if he or she becomes confined to a wheelchair? Or will you rationalize your way out of the relationship because staying with your mate would be impossible? You may not know the answer but you should make the effort to find it. At some point we all encounter our own wheelchairs, in the form of crises, illnesses, physical or mental changes, and we need someone loving to be there. Loving comes with *moral responsibility* and there is no true love without it. Your *moral responsibility* may end when your partner's conduct causes you to compromise your own morals and ethics.

As for getting a little help from "Above," it does not matter whether you subscribe to a particular religion. Just read the Ten Commandments, all of which encourage *mutual respect* and *moral responsibility.* Above all they require you to do your utmost to become *fit to love.* Even if the Ten Commandments are meaningless to you, you could never be wrong living by them. If you put love before every thought and every action, you will never have to question yourself or have any regrets.

Every mainstream religion has love at its core; only our arbitrary human interpretations of various religions can distort this fact.

Buddhism defines loves as wanting the other person's total happiness, even when we are not the one who can give it. That is another tall order, especially considering that we often wish the one who stops loving us "hell on earth." Even if we are not spiritually inclined, love is everywhere. We cannot escape it. While I do not want to preach to you (well, maybe a little), I believe we could all use some guidance from a higher spirit. Maybe as humans we are not strong enough on our own to love unconditionally. People have sought spiritual advice for thousands of years and many have reportedly found answers as well as their loving core within. This advice is free for the asking, always available and it will never fail. People have loved unconditionally for thousands of years, even before the invention of lingerie and romantic candlelight. Don't get me wrong, I love romance; however with five hundred candles burning in the bedroom and no true love, the Fire Department will get there long before true passion.

> *Love is patient, love is kind. It does not envy, it does not boast, it is not proud. It is not rude, it is not self-seeking, it is not easily angered, it keeps no record of wrongs. Love does not delight in evil but rejoices with the truth. It always protects, always trusts, always hopes, always perseveres. Love never fails.*
> —CORINTHIANS 13:4–8

People who love unconditionally are not afraid of what comes next. They do not fear change, aging, loss or even death because they never have to be afraid of having missed anything.

They also know that unconditional love, including self-love, comes with sacrifices. One must forego indulging in today's fast food love: quickly, impurely and cheaply!

> *To those who feel—Life is a Tragedy!*
> *To those who think—It is a Farce!*
> *To those who love—It is Real!*
> —AUTHOR UNKNOWN

❤ Love, the Universal Cure

A Columbine student wrote the following e-mail after the terrible shooting at his high school. I could not have written it better myself:

> *The paradox of our time in history is that we have taller buildings, but shorter tempers; wider freeways, but narrower viewpoints; we spend more, but enjoy less. We have bigger houses and smaller families; more conveniences, but less time; we have more degrees, but less sense; more knowledge, but less judgment; more experts, but less solutions; more medicine, but less wellness. We have multiplied our possessions, but reduced our values. We talk too much, love too seldom and hate too often. We have learned to make a living, but not a life; we've added years to life, not life to years. We've been all the way to the moon and back, but have trouble crossing the street to meet a new neighbor. We have conquered outer-space, but not-inner space; we've cleaned up the air, but polluted the soul; we've split the atom, but not our prejudice. We have higher incomes, but lower morals; we've become long on quantity, but short on quality. These are the times of tall men and short characters; steep profits and shallow relation-*

ships. These are the times of world peace, but domestic warfare, more leisure, but less fun. These are the days of two incomes, but more divorce, of fancier houses, but broken homes. It is a time when there is much in the show window and nothing in the stockroom; a time when technology can bring this letter to you, and a time when you can choose to either forward this message and make a difference...or just hit delete.

Today people earn more money, have more food, better employment, better housing, safer cars, more leisure pursuits, more TV channels, more access to information, live longer and have more distractions than ever before. Yet crime and suicide rates are rising and alcoholism and substance abuse are growing. Depression and other mental illnesses seem to be escalating and numerous publications allege that our nation today is less content and more stressed than ever before. We are running out of energy, feeling exhausted and psychologically malnourished. Nationwide, people are popping pick-me-up pills, submitting to miracle therapies and are absorbed in many trivial distractions in an effort to suffer less. We evaluate each other on the basis of our material possessions and in our quest to live up to societal dogma, we have been coached into being the ultimate consumers.

As a consequence, we acquire and consume anything and grow to be less fulfilled in our lives. In our self-absorbed perception, we seek instantaneous gratification and quick fixes. Regardless of our profoundly deep longing for love, we seem to place more importance on money, power, status, inanimate things and accomplishments than we do on love. Even though our nation is in need of love more than anything else, we look for solutions elsewhere. Moreover, we do not hear the voices of our children, the upcoming generation, who urgently need our support in creating a better world.

Love is the supreme energy behind all acts of humanity. There would be no food for the hungry if not for the love of the famished, no ecological movements if not for the love of nature, no churches if not for the love of God, no child and youth organizations if not for the love of the dependent, and no books, such as this one, if not for the love of sharing wisdom. No matter how much we agree or disagree with their causes, all of the above began in the name of love. Everything good on this planet transpires through the potent strength of love and all evil stems from its absence.

Love has the power to transform our planet and people everywhere are joining this liberating movement, for love is truly freedom.

> *Love is the only force capable of transforming an enemy into a friend.*
> —Martin Luther King, Jr.

If we simply let love guide us in everything we do, we would never make mistakes and would proudly accept responsibility for the world that we shape. While, in our lifetime, we are unlikely to see all human beings as friends, we must nevertheless fuel this planet with love and lead by example.

> *Many ask God: "Why don't you do anything about the evil on this earth?"*
> *God answers: "I was just about to ask you the same thing."*
> —Author Unknown

Are you ready to do something? You do not have to become a large-scale crusader or rebel to make a difference. Instead, revolutionize your thoughts and make your own world more loving. If you are in a relationship, love with your whole heart and show it. If you are searching for love, be patient and give another person a chance. Above all, do not turn your back on love every time it touches you, because when you give up on love you give up on yourself.

Whatever you have done in the past can never be as important as what you will do today. Today is a great day to step out in love because you are given another chance to try a little harder. Try a little harder each day and before you know it, you will be *fit to love*. Even though most of the decisions in this world are made in the name of profit and gains, try to make yours in the name of love. Love has so many more solutions than it does problems and we all have enough love inside to be part of the solution.

A loving heart is the truest wisdom.
—CHARLES DICKENS

On the morning of the September 11, 2001 attack, thousands went to work at the World Trade Center, humans who loved and were loved. All believed that September 11, 2001, would be just another ordinary day in their lives: going to work, commuting home, having dinner, maybe going to the gym, helping their children with homework, sharing some wine with their spouse, watching TV and everything else people do. They also believed that there would be a tomorrow.

As one man, who became a widower because of the attack, said:

> *I wish that I had told my wife more often how much I loved her, needed her and how grateful I was to have her in my life. I would give anything to see her smile one more time, touch her warm skin again, hold her close to me and feel the love, safety and comfort. But never again, for now her skin is cold, her smile lifeless and her breath extinguished forever. I wish I would have, while I still had the time. Instead, I was chasing the big dream of material accomplishments and failed to seize the moment.*

Never take anything or anyone for granted. Not even a day, a moment or yourself. We all have a Mac truck to worry about and for some of us the Mack truck is speeding our way. It is the small, meaningful interactions you share with your loved ones that make your life spectacular and your memories priceless.

Conclusion

It took many dedicated love-crusaders to bring this book into your hands. Single or not, they gave me encouragement, compassion and lots of information. I am sure, after listening patiently to my discussions, many people are relieved to find this book completed and quite happy to take a break from me (until the next book: *Are You Fit to . . . ?*). Some have threatened to change their e-mail addresses, just to escape me. Nevertheless, I am grateful to all who wrote to me about what love means to them.

You might have decided to read this book for many reasons. Among them, you wanted to find love, you wanted your relationship to be more meaningful or you were ready for the truth about love. This book will, hopefully, have helped you to change your beliefs about love and become brave enough to experience it on your own. The intention of this book is for all of us to grow into mature, morally responsible people of integrity, for only then can we collectively embrace the real power of love. In order for our love to have real power we need to change our hearts and lives, by consciously exercising *mutual respect* and *moral responsibility*. This is the force that drives unconditional love. It contains commitment, trust, integrity and selflessness. Once you can unconditionally love another person, you can love the entire world. This is also the time, when true peace finds its way into your heart. You are then *Fit to Love*.

> *It is said that to have really loved one person is to have loved the whole world.*
> —BARRY NEIL KAUFMAN (1977)

❤ 5 Principles to Remember from Chapter Ten

1. *Moral responsibility* means being aware that everything you do or say affects those around you.
2. *Mutual respect* also means becoming better for each other.
3. If you do not stand up for love, you don't stand for much of anything.
4. Nothing you or I do in our lives will ever matter as much as the way we love.
5. If you give up on love, you give up on yourself.

www.areyoufittolove.com

APPENDIX

Company Information

Single Again MAGAZINE ONLINE
Website: www.singleagain.com
Contact: Rev. Paul Scholl, publisher
Phone: USA, 916-773-7337
E-mail: publisher@singleagain.com

REALCAFES.COM INC.
Websites: www.christiancafe.com, www.jewishcafe.com
www.barbrasil.com, www.catholiccafe.com
Contact: Sam and Philip Moorcroft
Phone: Canada, 905-326-8094
E-mail: info@realcafes.com

ELLEN REID'S BOOK SHEPHERDING, A DIVISION OF SMARKETING
Website: www.smarketing.com
Contact: Ellen Reid
Phone: Beverly Hills, CA 310-234-0626
Toll Free: 866-406-4352
E-mail: ellen@smarketing.com

COOMBS'S CREATIVE SERVICE
Contact: Samm H. Coombs
Phone: Palm Desert, CA 760-674-4474
Email: scoombs@dc.rr.com

SIMONE GABBAY, AUTHOR AND EDITOR
Website: www.pathcom.com\~egabbay
Phone: Toronto, 416-446-0862
E-mail: sgabbay@pathcom.com

EDITING INK COMMUNICATION SERVICES
Contact: Susana Gomes
Phone: Newcastle, 905-987-1589
E-mail: editingink@rogers.com

ALBERTINE GRAPHIC DESIGN
Contact: Dotti Albertine
Phone: Beverly Hills, CA 310-278-8810
E-mail: dotti@dotdesign.net
Website: www.dotdesign.net

BIBLIOGRAPHY

Buscaglia, Leo. 1972. *Love: What Life Is All About.* New York: Ballantine Books.

Coombs, Samm. 1995. *Time Happens.* San Francisco: Halo Books.

Darwin, Charles. 1859. *On the Origin of Species.* Reprinted by various publishers.

DeAngelis, Barbara. 1992. *Are You the One for Me?* New York: Dell Publishing.

Dyer, Wayne. 1995. *Your Sacred Self.* New York: Harper Paperbacks.

Erikson, Erik H. 1994. *Identity and the Life Cycle.* New York: W.W. Norton & Company.

Fein, Ellen and Sherrie Schneider. 1997. *Rules II: More Rules to Live and Love By.* New York: AOL Time Warner Book Group.

Fox-Genovese, Elizabeth. 1991. *Feminism without Illusions: A Critique of Individualism.* Chapel Hill, NC: University of North Carolina Press.

Fromm, Erich. 1961. *Marx's Concept of Man.* New York: Frederick Ungar Publishing Company.

Fromm, Erich. 1956. *The Art of Loving.* New York: Harper Perennial.

Goffman, Eving. 1959. *Presentation of Self in Everyday Life.* New York: Doubleday Anchor.

Hare, John E. 1996. *The Moral Gap: Kantian Ethics, Human Limits, and God's Assistance.* Oxford, UK: Oxford University.

Hendrix, Harville. 2001. *Getting the Love You Want: A Guide for Couples.* New York: Henry Holt and Company.

Kaufman, Barry N. 1991. *Happiness Is a Choice.* New York: Ballantine Books.

Larson, Hal & Suzie. 1993. *Suddenly Single.* San Francisco: Halo Books.

Larson, Hal. 1994. *If He Loves Me, Why Doesn't He Tell Me.* San Francisco: Halo Books.

MacNabb, D.G.C. 1951. *David Hume, His Theory of Knowledge and Morality.* London, UK: Hutchinson's University Library.

McGraw, Phillip. 2001. *Relationship Rescue: A Seven-Step Strategy for Reconnecting with Your Partner.* New York: Hyperion Press.

McGraw, Phillip. 2002. *Self-Matters: Creating Your Life from the Inside Out.* New York: Simon & Schuster.

McGraw, Phillip. 1999. *Life Strategies.* New York: Hyperion Press.

Mishra, Ramesh. 1990. *The Welfare State in Capitalist Society.* Toronto: University of Toronto Press.

Page, Susan. 1988. *If I'm So Wonderful, Why Am I Still Single?* New York: Viking.

Page, Susan. 1997. *How One of You Can Bring the Two of You Together: Breakthrough Strategies to Resolve Your Conflicts and Re-Ignite Your Love.* New York: Broadway Books.

Real, Terrence. 2002. *How Can I Get Through to You: Reconnecting Men and Women.* New York: Scribner.

Roazzi, Vincent M. 2002. *The Spirituality of Success: Getting Rich with Integrity.* Dallas: Brown Books.

Ruiz, Don Miguel. 1999. *Mastery of Love: A Practical Guide to the Art of Relationship.* San Rafael, CA: Amber-Allen Publishing.

Schmaltz, Tad M. 1996. *Malebranche's Theory of the Soul: A Cartesian Interpretation.* New York: Oxford University Press.

Skinner, B. F. 2002. *Beyond Freedom and Dignity . . . 1971.* Indianapolis: Hackett Publishing Company (reprint).

Weiner-Davis, Michele. 1993. *Divorce Busting: A Revolutionary and Rapid Program for Staying Together.* New York: Simon & Schuster.

Weiner-Davis, Michele. 2001. *Divorce Remedy: The Proven 7-Step Program for Saving Your Marriage.* New York: Simon & Schuster.

Welwood, John. 1990. *Journey of the Heart: Intimate Relationships and the Path of Love.* New York: Harper Perennial.

"Psychiatry: Cases of Fraud." *Betraying Society: A Publication by the Citizens Commission on Human Rights. 1999.* Los Angeles, CA.

How To Engage Allie Ochs, Speaker & Author

Website: www.areyoufittolove.com

E-mail: allie@areyoufittolove.com

By Mail: Ellen Reid, Publisher
Little Moose Press
269 So. Beverly Dr., #1065
Beverly Hills, CA 90212
TEL 310-446-3005
TOLL-FREE 866-234-0626
FAX 310-278-6238
www.littlemoosepress.com
info@littlemoosepress.com

To order: www.areyoufittolove.com or 1-866-234-0626

Relationship Coaching

If you have tried everything to either turn your relationship around or to find love, don't give up hope. Individual or couple relationship coaching with Allie based on the *Are You Fit to Love* principles is available on our website. Please check: www.areyoufittolove.com for your choice of personal or on-line coaching.

Workshops and Seminars

Allie Ochs is available for corporate/private workshops, seminars, coaching or keynote presentations. She delivers a series of relationship programs designed to radically improve all types of relationships. Inquire about how Allie can effectively structure a series of relationship programs specific to your situation. Please visit our website: www.areyoufittolove.com for details or e-mail: info@areyoufittolove.com

Please visit our website, share your ideas, comments, dreams and hopes. Reach out and meet like-minded individuals. Watch for new books addressing all types of relationships. Your help is needed in creating meaningful relationships, which subsequently lead to a better world. Get in touch with us. We are just like you and look forward to hearing from you.

The collective power of love is everywhere!
Don't sit on the fence – do something!

ORDER FORM

LITTLE MOOSE PRESS
269 So. Beverly Drive, #1065
Beverly Hills, CA 90212

Please send me the following:

QUAN.	ITEM	PRICE
_____	*Fit to Love* / Paperback $15.95 ea. / $19.95 (Canada)	_____
	(Deduct 10% discount for five or more)	_____
	SUBTOTAL	_____
	(CA residents add 8.25%) SALES TAX	_____
	($3.50 for first book, then $.50 for each add'l book) SHIPPING	_____
	TOTAL	_____

NAME

COMPANY NAME

ADDRESS

MAILING ADDRESS *(IF DIFFERENT FROM ABOVE)*

CITY   STATE   ZIP

HOME TELEPHONE   FAX   EMAIL

PAYMENT:

❑ Checks payable to *Little Moose Press* and mail to:
269 So. Beverly Dr., #1065, Beverly Hills, CA 90212

❑ VISA ❑ MasterCard ❑ AMEX ❑ Discover

Cardnumber:_____
Name on card:_____
Exp. Date: _____(mo) _____(year)

■ Toll free order phone 866-234-0626 (secure message machine). Give mailing/shipping address, telephone number, MC/Visa name & card number plus expiration date.
■ Secure Fax orders: 310-278-6238. Fill out this form & fax.
■ On-line orders: www.areyoufittolove.com
orders@areyoufittolove.com

www.areyoufittolove.com